Our **Planet** Today

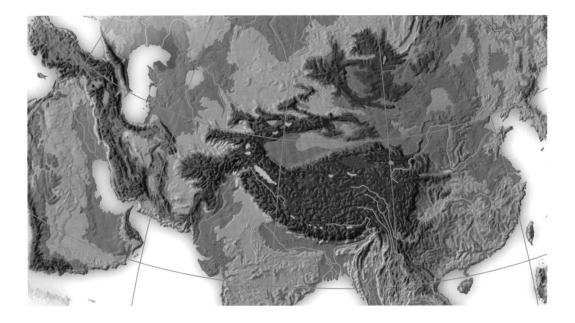

WORLD ALMANAC® LIBRARY

Please visit our web site at: www.worldalmanaclibrary.com
For a free color catalog describing World Almanac® Library's list of high-quality books
and multimedia programs, call 1-800-848-2928 (USA) or 1-800-461-9120 (Canada).
World Almanac® Library's Fax: (414) 332-3567.

The editors at World Almanac® Library would like to thank Paul Mayer, Geology Collections
Manager, Milwaukee Public Museum, for the technical expertise and advice he brought to
the production of this book.

Library of Congress Cataloging-in-Publication Data

Our planet today. — North American ed.
     p. cm. — (21st century science)
     Includes bibliographical references and index.
     ISBN 0-8368-5003-3 (lib. bdg.)
     1. Landforms—Juvenile literature. 2. Continents—Juvenile literature. 3. Cartography—
Juvenile literature. [1. Landforms. 2. Continents.] I. Title. II. Series.
     QB406.O87 2001
     551.41—dc21   2001031093

This North American edition first published in 2001 by
World Almanac® Library
330 West Olive Street, Suite 100
Milwaukee, WI 53212 USA

Created and produced as the *Visual Guide to Understanding the Earth* by
     QA INTERNATIONAL
     329 rue de la Commune Ouest, 3ᵉ étage
     Montreal, Québec
     Canada H2Y 2E1

     Tel: (514) 499-3000 Fax: (514) 499-3010
     www.qa-international.com

     © QA International, 2001

               Editorial Director: François Fortin
Executive Editor: Serge D'Amico
Art Director: Rielle Lévesque
Graphic Designer: Anne Tremblay
Writers: Nathalie Fredette, Stéphane Batigne, Josée Bourbonnière, Claude Lafleur,
Agence Science-Presse
Computer Graphic Artists: Jean-Yves Ahern, Maxime Bigras, Patrice Blais, Yan Bohler,
Mélanie Boivin, Charles Campeau, Jocelyn Gardner, Jonathan Jacques, Alain Lemire,
Raymond Martin, Nicolas Oroc, Carl Pelletier, Simon Pelletier, Frédérick Simard,
Mamadou Togola, Yan Tremblay
Page Layout: Lucie Mc Brearty, Véronique Boisvert, Geneviève Théroux Béliveau
Researchers: Anne-Marie Villeneuve, Anne-Marie Brault, Kathleen Wynd, Jessie Daigle
Earth Reviewer: Michèle Fréchet
Copy Editor: Liliane Michaud
Production: Mac Thien Nguyen Hoang
Prepress: Tony O'Riley
World Almanac® Library Editor: David K. Wright
World Almanac® Library Art Direction: Karen Knutson
Cover Design: Katherine A. Kroll

Photo credits: abbreviations: t = top, c = center, b = bottom, r = right, l = left
p. 7 (tr): Joel W. Rogers/CORBIS/Magma; pp. 8 (br), 11 (tr): David Muench/CORBIS/Magma;
p. 14 (cl): William A. Bake/CORBIS/Magma; p. 15 (tl): Nathan Benn/CORBIS/Magma; p. 29
(t): © 1984 Her Majesty the Queen in Right of Canada, reproduced from the collection of the
National Air Photo Library with permission of National Resources Canada; p. 36 (tl): Hulton-
Deutsch Collection/CORBIS/Magma; p. 36 (cr): www.ccrs.nrcan.gc.ca; p. 36 (br): USGS; p. 37
(br): Felix Kogan/NOAA/NESDIS; p. 38 (tl & cl): Radarsat Images © 1996. Courtesy of the
Canadian Space Agency. Acquired by the CSA. Received by the CCRS. Processed by RSI; p. 39
(br): Courtesy of NASA/JPL/Caltech; p. 41 (tr): National Maritime Museum, London; p. 45
(bl): Dr. John Anderson, Rice University, Dept. of Geology & Geophysics; p. 46 (cr): Richard
Hamilton Smith/CORBIS/Magma; p. 46 (br): Liz Hymans/CORBIS/Magma; p. 47 (br): Danny
Lehman/CORBIS/Magma; pp. 48 (cr), 57 (tr): Wolfgang Kaehler/CORBIS/Magma; p. 49 (tr):
James Marshall/CORBIS/Magma; p. 51 (cl): Michael Buselle/CORBIS/Magma; pp. 51 (b), 56
(c): Tiziana and Gianni Baldizzone; p. 53 (tr): WildCountry/CORBIS/Magma; p. 53 (cr): Earl &
Nazima Kowall/CORBIS/Magma; p. 53 (bl): Julia Waterlow; Eye Ubiquitous/CORBIS/Magma;
pp. 54 (cr), 55 (tl): Yann Arthus-Bertrand/CORBIS/Magma; p. 57 (c):
Nik Wheeler/CORBIS/Magma; p. 57 (br): Sharna Balfour; Gallo Images/CORBIS/Magma

Printed in Canada

1 2 3 4 5 6 7 8 9 05 04 03 02 01

Table of Contents

While mountains result from large-scale tectonic movements, the landscape changes much more quietly from day to day. All around us, valleys are being carved out, dunes are accumulating, hills are flattening, caves are opening. Thanks to slow, steady erosion by water, wind, and ice, Earth's surface is constantly evolving to form a stunning diversity of landscapes.

The Evolving Landscape

Erosion

Mechanisms that transform landscapes

Landscapes that seem the same from day to day are actually in a state of constant change. Spectacular events, such as volcanic eruptions and floods, change Earth's topography in sometimes radical ways, but erosion, though much more discreet, is one of the main mechanisms in the transformation of Earth's relief features.

Erosion, a process involving wearing down, altering, and leveling, is a cycle that begins with the gradual removal of surface materials and continues with the transportation of eroded particles (sediments) until they are deposited.

DIFFERENT TYPES OF EROSION

Water, wind, and ice are the main agents of erosion. They profoundly alter the landscape through chemical and mechanical processes.

EROSION BY INFILTRATION

Water **runoff** moves particles of soil and digs out ravines.

EROSION BY WAVES

Cliffs are sculpted by sea **waves**. Rocks are made fragile by the abrasive and chemical action of salt and algae and are altered under the repeated impact of swells and tides.

deltaic deposits

oceanic deposits

FLUVIAL EROSION

River water scours materials from the banks and riverbed, rolling them against each other and fragmenting them. These particles have an abrasive effect that carves out riverbanks.

fluvial deposits

lagunal deposits

AN EXAMPLE OF LANDSCAPE ALTERATION: MONOLITHS

In some regions, the wind violently blows grains of sand onto rocks, acting as an abrasive. Over millennia, this form of erosion creates unusually shaped monoliths, such as those in Monument Valley, Arizona.

GLACIAL EROSION

Glaciers that scrape the slopes of high mountains perform a form of mechanical alteration. Thanks to gravity, an **ice tongue** spreads down the mountain. As it descends, this mass of ice carries rock fragments, pebbles, and sand, carving out a valley as it goes.

CONGELIFRACTION

Water increases in volume by about 10 percent when it freezes. If this takes place in a tight crack in a rock, the rock is subjected to enormous pressure that literally splits it apart. Congelifraction occurs in mountains where **frosts** and thaws alternate.

FLUVIAL EROSION

Loaded with carbon dioxide from the atmosphere, and sometimes with sulfur dioxide, **rainwater** chemically alters various minerals present in the ground, including limestone. The stone erodes on its surface and along the cracks.

boulder clays

deposits left by flash floods

EOLIAN EROSION

Wind makes its mark, particularly on plains and deserts. Land where grains of sand are exposed to the wind is gradually worn away.

dunes

The Cycle of Erosion

The effects of time on the landscape

The cycle of erosion takes place at various speeds, but most are imperceptibly slow on a human scale: a fissure in a block of granite generally widens by only a fraction of an inch (or a few millimeters) in one thousand years. Massifs, semi-arid regions, and zones where the surface of the land has been modified by human activity (such as clear-cutting or construction of roads and cities) obviously experience the most rapid erosion. The slowest erosion is associated with lowlands where materials are very hard, such as the Canadian Shield.

THE EVOLUTION OF A LANDSCAPE

Relief features go through a series of successive stages. Fluvial landscapes are altered by the eroding action of watercourses.

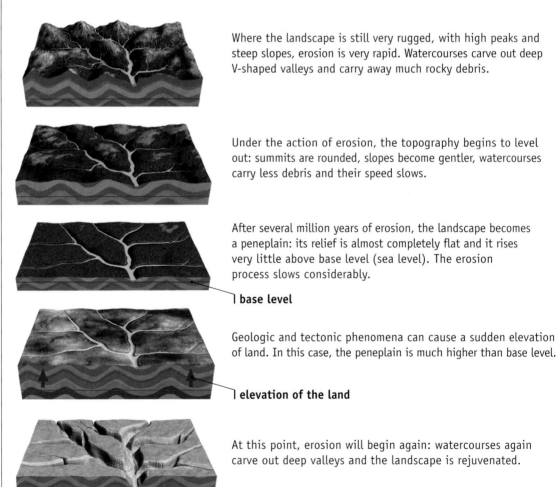

Where the landscape is still very rugged, with high peaks and steep slopes, erosion is very rapid. Watercourses carve out deep V-shaped valleys and carry away much rocky debris.

Under the action of erosion, the topography begins to level out: summits are rounded, slopes become gentler, watercourses carry less debris and their speed slows.

After several million years of erosion, the landscape becomes a peneplain: its relief is almost completely flat and it rises very little above base level (sea level). The erosion process slows considerably.

⌐ **base level**

Geologic and tectonic phenomena can cause a sudden elevation of land. In this case, the peneplain is much higher than base level.

⌐ **elevation of the land**

At this point, erosion will begin again: watercourses again carve out deep valleys and the landscape is rejuvenated.

THE COLORADO RIVER GRAND CANYON

The elevation of the Colorado plateau in Arizona led to the carving out of deep gorges. To return to its base level, the Colorado River sank by broadening its bed, carving out canyons up to .9 mile (1.5 kilometer) deep.

Landslides

When weight shapes the landscape

Landslides help to shape the landscape — sometimes slowly, sometimes quickly, and sometimes very suddenly. They are triggered by major climatic change (frost, thaw, torrential rain), actions that upset the balance of the soil (deforestation, construction), or tremors (earthquakes, volcanic eruptions). Landslides are a special form of erosion, linked to Earth's gravity. Depending on the incline of the slope, the nature of the soil, and the triggering element, these phenomena, also called mass movements, may take various forms: creeps, earthflows, avalanches, and landslips.

CREEPS AND EARTHFLOW

By impregnating the materials of a slope, water and snow reduce the cohesion of particles of earth and rock, making them easily mobile.

A **mudflow** is among the most fluid and rapid mass movements. It occurs mainly in arid and semi-arid regions, when torrential rains rapidly saturate the ground. The mud flows down natural ravines and spreads at the foot of the slope.

An **earthflow** occurs when the upper part of a piece of land yields and descends, forming a tongue of earth of varying lengths. This phenomenon occurs most frequently among clay and schistose soils in humid regions.

A mass movement that is imperceptibly slow, **creep** affects the landscape nevertheless. Bent trees, leaning poles, and sagging walls attest to the moving of the upper layer of ground. Humidity alternating with dryness is the main cause of creep.

AVALANCHES

Very steep slopes can be the site of the free fall of pieces of earth or rocks.

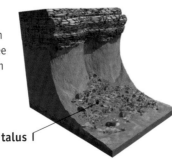

talus

LANDSLIPS

Landslips carry materials (earth or rocks) along one or several surfaces.

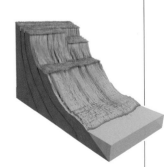

A **rockslide** is a sudden fall of stones, broken apart by frost or by plant roots. This phenomenon occurs mainly along canyons, cliffs, and mountain roads. The accumulation of stones at the foot of rock faces forms a talus.

A **rotational slip** occurs when part of a slope slides along a curved or concave surface. This phenomenon, which affects poorly consolidated soil, may be caused by erosion at the base of a slope (river or waves) or by the addition of weight.

Caves

Excavations sculpted by water

Underground cavities are found all over the planet: in cliffs overhanging the ocean, in solidified lava, and even in glaciers. Porous rocks, such as limestone and dolomite, contain the largest networks of caves. These natural excavations, which stretch out horizontally (galleries) or vertically (potholes, shafts), are the result of water's slow erosion of the bedrock. It takes tens of thousands of years to form a cave a few feet (a few meters) in diameter and almost 100 years for a stalactite, a mass of calcite pointing down toward the ground, to grow 2 inches (5 centimeters)!

FORMATION OF A CAVE

1. As it infiltrates the rock, naturally acid rainwater dissolves the limestone and slowly widens existing cracks.

2. When it reaches the groundwater, water flows horizontally toward a natural outlet, slowly carving out galleries.

3. As water continues to hollow out the bedrock, the groundwater gradually drops, causing the upper gallery to dry out and become a fossil gallery.

Lapiés are large flat areas that have had grooves carved into them by chemical erosion of the limestone.

Steep openings called sinkholes or **potholes** form at the surface when the vault of a cave collapses.

old groundwater level

Calcite (calcium carbonate) is deposited in the form of small step-shaped barriers called **gours**.

Groundwater, fed by rainwater that infiltrates the bedrock, slowly circulates, impregnating the rock.

shaft

lake

When stalactites and stalagmites meet, they form **columns**.

VAST NETWORKS

Caves are organized in networks that may extend great distances. What is believed to be the world's largest underground group of caves, Mammoth Cave, is in Kentucky; this network of galleries stretches more than 340 miles (550 km).

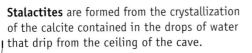

Stalactites are formed from the crystallization of the calcite contained in the drops of water that drip from the ceiling of the cave.

The constant infiltration of water into rock forms funnel-shaped depressions 100–325 feet (30–100 m) across called **dolines**.

Stalagmites seem to grow out of the ground. In fact, they result from crystallization of the calcite in the water drops that fall from the vault of the cave or from stalactites.

Gorges are often the result of the collapse of the vaults of a network of caves.

waterfall

scree

When an underground stream resurfaces, it is called a **resurgence**.

underground river

fossil gallery

How Mountains Are Formed

Complex geologic processes

The uplifting of Earth's surface, or emergence, is the result of complex processes: a single mountain chain may be composed of metamorphic rocks, remnants of oceanic crust, and volcanic rocks. These different types of rocks are generally arranged in strata, which have been folded, inverted, or even dislocated along fault lines.

The discovery of plate tectonics allowed great steps to be made in our understanding of orogeny (the process of mountain formation). In fact, most mountains are the result of the movement of oceanic and continental plates.

BETWEEN OCEAN AND CONTINENT

When an oceanic plate ❶ collides with a continent ❷, it slips ❸ under the continental plate. Oceanic sediments scraped off by this contact accumulate in an accretionary wedge ❹. As the oceanic plate sinks, the volume of the accretionary wedge increases; sometimes, it rises well above sea level and forms coastal mountains ❺. The continental plate, subjected to considerable force, folds and buckles, giving rise to a chain of subduction mountains ❻. When the oceanic plate reaches the mantle, its rocks melt and become magma ❼. These molten rocks sometimes rise to the surface and are ejected by volcanoes ❽.

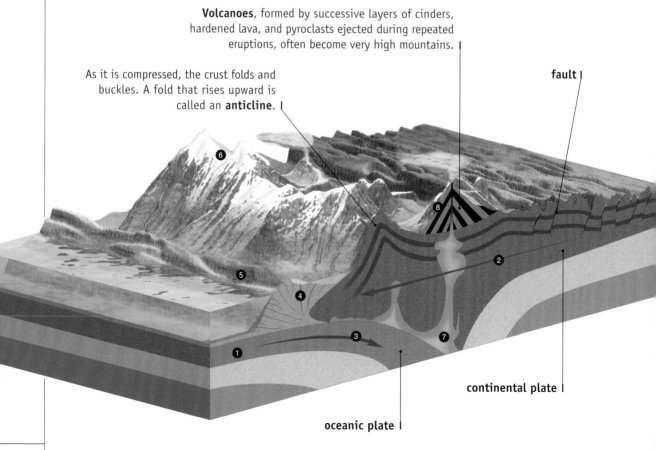

Volcanoes, formed by successive layers of cinders, hardened lava, and pyroclasts ejected during repeated eruptions, often become very high mountains.

As it is compressed, the crust folds and buckles. A fold that rises upward is called an **anticline**.

fault

continental plate

oceanic plate

WHEN CONTINENTS COLLIDE

The collision of two continental plates causes such a huge shock that there are major geological upheavals. A collision of this type 53 million years ago gave rise to the Himalayas, the highest mountain chain in the world. When two continental plates ❶ come into contact, they press on each other, deforming ❷ and overlapping one another. Bedrock raised by this movement folds and forms a chain of collision mountains ❸.

Sedimentary rock strata are sometimes folded and pushed up to very great heights by the collision of plates.

A **suture** is the border between two continental plates.

continental plates

dome

DOME MOUNTAINS

Magma that rises toward Earth's surface accumulates in gigantic magmatic chambers. If the molten rock is not ejected by a volcanic eruption, it raises the rocky strata on the surface into dome shapes.

magma

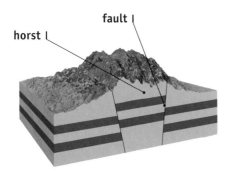

fault

horst

HORSTS

Tensions and pressures exerted on the plates may cause faults to appear, along which blocks of rock slide and are displaced. Horsts are blocks that are uplifted. Sometimes, they are big enough to be mountains.

Mountains of the World

Evidence of tectonic activity

A mountain's appearance depends in great part on its age. The youngest mountain chains on the planet (the Alps, Himalayas, Rockies, Andes, Caucasus) have a very marked relief, with steep slopes and sharp peaks. Most of them have not finished rising, as slow-moving tectonic plates continue to deform the landscape. The oldest mountains (Urals, Appalachians, the Great Dividing Range in Australia, Drakensberg Mountains) are less rugged looking: they have been smoothed by erosion, which has taken material from the slopes and deposited it in the hollows.

OLD MOUNTAINS

Formed more than 300 million years ago, the **Appalachians** are among the oldest mountains in the world. Their relief shows the low progress of erosion by ice, wind, and water, which have softened the angles of their peaks and slopes.

The **Rockies** were uplifted by subduction along the west coast of North America. They are bordered by a coastal chain that is the result of the uplifting of a sedimentary accretionary wedge.

The **Sierra Nevada** are block mountains consisting of horsts.

The longest mountain chain in the world is the **Andes**: this chain stretches for almost 8,000 miles (12,880 km) north to south. The southern part (Chile, Argentina), which includes the highest peaks in the chain, was formed by subduction of the Pacific plate under South America.

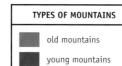

TYPES OF MOUNTAINS
old mountains
young mountains

MOUNTAINS IN EQUILIBRIUM

The higher the mountain, the deeper its roots extend into Earth's mantle ❶. As it erodes, its mass diminishes. Like a ship whose waterline rises when its cargo is removed, the mountain is uplifted. At the same time, accumulations of sedimentary deposits around the mountain force the crust to sink into the mantle ❷. This compensation effect is called isostasy.

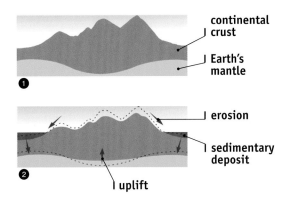

continental crust

Earth's mantle

erosion

sedimentary deposit

❷

uplift

YOUNG MOUNTAINS

The high peaks and steep slopes of the **Alps** are evidence of this mountain chain's youth. Its rugged relief was probably produced about 50 million years ago, when the Eurasian plate collided with the African plate.

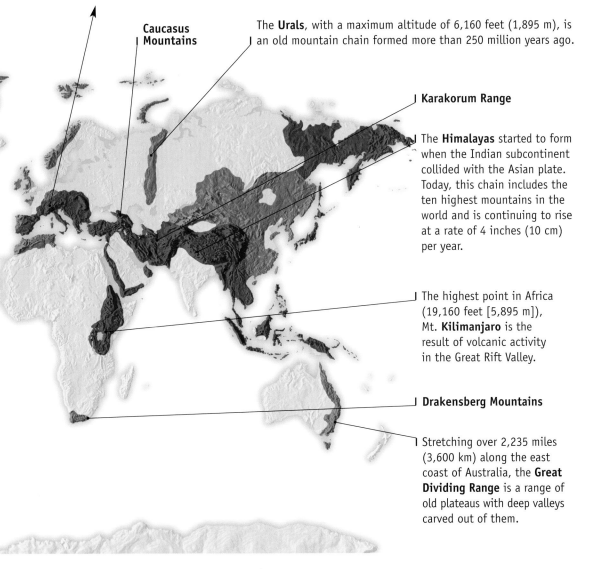

Caucasus Mountains

The **Urals**, with a maximum altitude of 6,160 feet (1,895 m), is an old mountain chain formed more than 250 million years ago.

Karakorum Range

The **Himalayas** started to form when the Indian subcontinent collided with the Asian plate. Today, this chain includes the ten highest mountains in the world and is continuing to rise at a rate of 4 inches (10 cm) per year.

The highest point in Africa (19,160 feet [5,895 m]), Mt. **Kilimanjaro** is the result of volcanic activity in the Great Rift Valley.

Drakensberg Mountains

Stretching over 2,235 miles (3,600 km) along the east coast of Australia, the **Great Dividing Range** is a range of old plateaus with deep valleys carved out of them.

Configuration of the Coastline

Between sea and land

The littoral zone is the coastal area between the low- and high-tide levels. Shorelines are in perpetual transformation, thanks to the constant action of the sea, rivers, and wind. They take a wide variety of forms, depending on the geologic nature of the coast.

There are two types of coasts. A shoreline of submergence is eroded by waves, which hit the rocky cliffs with considerable force (about 3 tons per cubic yard [per m³] and up to about 50 tons per cubic yard [per m³] during storms). The rocks broken off from the coast are ground into finer particles, which are deposited on the coasts and mix with river sediments to shape another type of littoral zone, an accumulation shoreline of progradation.

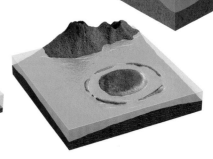

shoreline of submergence

FROM CLIFF TO REEF

Depending on the type of rock they are made of, some parts of the coast erode more quickly. For instance, cliffs ❶ jutting into the sea form capes ❷. The water carves out this exposed area and transforms a crack into a cave ❸. When two caves become joined on either side of the cape, they create an arch ❹. As it collapses, the arch leaves a needle ❺, which is later transformed into an islet or a reef ❻.

Where the bedrock is softest, the shoreline forms a hollow that is called a **bay**.

DIFFERENT TYPES OF SHORELINES

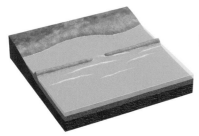

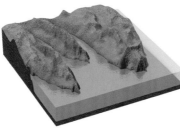

The **barrier beach** (barrier island) is a sandbar parallel to the shore at a distance of several miles (several km). Between the barrier and the shore is a lagoon.

Fjords ("long arm of the sea" in Norwegian) are valleys that were carved out long ago by glaciers, then invaded by water. They are found on the Norwegian coast.

Some shorelines are the result of volcanic eruptions. The coral reef, or **atoll**, that forms around a volcanic island is in a ring shape surrounding a lagoon.

LONGSHORE DRIFT

The grains of sand and pebbles that are deposited on the coast do not stay put. They are moved by waves ❶, which push them obliquely along the shore ❷, drop them perpendicular to the coastline during backwash ❸, then carry them once more on a diagonal line ❹. This sawtooth pattern of movement, called longshore drift, ultimately creates a distinct series of sediment deposits ❺.

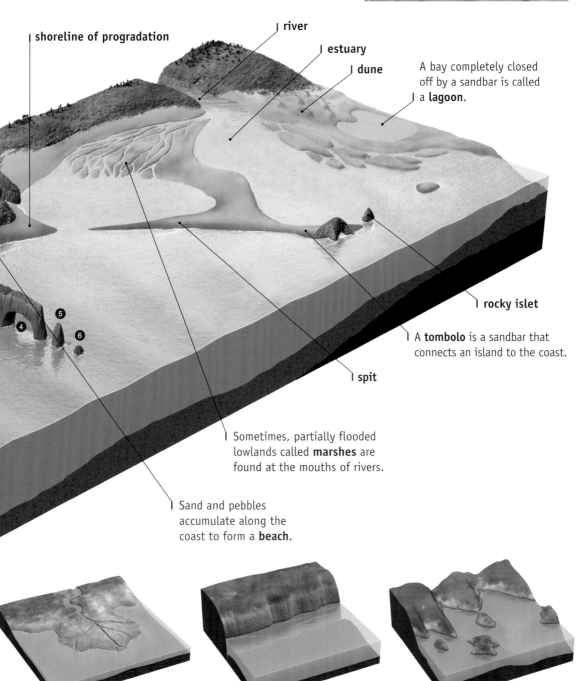

shoreline of progradation

river

estuary

dune

A bay completely closed off by a sandbar is called a **lagoon**.

rocky islet

A **tombolo** is a sandbar that connects an island to the coast.

spit

Sometimes, partially flooded lowlands called **marshes** are found at the mouths of rivers.

Sand and pebbles accumulate along the coast to form a **beach**.

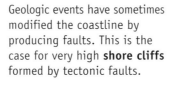

Deltas form at the mouths of rivers. They result from the accumulation and deposit of sediments carried by rivers flowing to the sea.

Geologic events have sometimes modified the coastline by producing faults. This is the case for very high **shore cliffs** formed by tectonic faults.

A fluvial valley submerged following a rise in sea level or a subsidence of land forms a group of coves called **rias** that indent the coast.

Glaciers

Rivers of ice

All regions that are constantly covered with snow, whether they are located close to the poles or at the tops of high mountains at any latitude, have glaciers. In fact, almost 10 percent of Earth's landmass (principally Antarctica and Greenland) is covered with these bodies of ice, which move under the force of their own weight. Mountain glaciers, several miles (several km) long and several dozen yards (several dozen m) thick, descend into the valleys at a speed of between 325 and 650 feet (100 and 200 m) per year. Their erosive action profoundly transforms landscapes, creating cirques, carving out flat-bottomed valleys, and depositing masses of rocks.

As it becomes detached from the rocky wall, the glacier leaves a deep crevice parallel to the rock face, a **bergschrund**.

The main glacier is often fed by **tributary glaciers**.

A **medial moraine** is formed where two ice streams meet.

valley glacier

The valley glacier sometimes retreats to form a **riegel**, characterized by a transversal rocky relief.

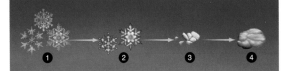

FROM SNOW TO ICE

Under pressure, the weight of accumulated snowflakes ❶ squeezes out the air, and the flakes become denser ❷. Lower temperatures cause melted crystals on the surface to refreeze and stick together ❸, and they are transformed into ice ❹. This metamorphosis takes many years (up to 3,500 in Antarctica) to complete.

A BALANCE BETWEEN PRECIPITATION AND MELTING

All glaciers are composed of two successive zones: the zone of accumulation, at the top of the glacier, and the zone of ablation, at the bottom. The equilibrium line, which separates the two zones, is clearly visible at the end of summer, when the top of the glacier is covered with fresh white snow, while its bottom part is composed of ice and darker old snow. In the Alps, this line is at 9,750 feet (3,000 m) altitude, but it is much higher in the Himalayas and the Andes.

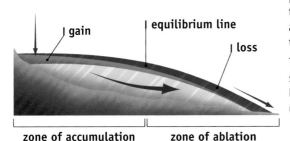

The glacier is in mass balance when gains of new snow in the zone of accumulation compensate for losses in the zone of ablation. When this balance is upset, the glacier retreats or advances.

THE EVOLUTION OF A VALLEY GLACIER

A glacier is born in a glacial cirque ❶, when the snow has accumulated, been compacted, and been transformed into ice. It flows down the slope ❷ under the force of gravity and invades the valley. As it descends, the glacier erodes the ground by scraping up rocks and debris ❸, which it drags under its mass; these materials increase its abrasive effect. The resulting friction slows the base of the glacier, while its surface moves more rapidly and is deformed, creating crevices ❹. As it descends, the main glacier is often joined by tributary glaciers ❺. When it reaches an altitude where the temperature is higher, the front of the glacier melts ❻, freeing rock debris that is deposited in moraines ❼. The meltwater forms streams and sometimes accumulates in a lake ❽ where a moraine has formed a dam.

Hanging glaciers remain in their cirques.

When the slope gets steeper, the surface of the glacier cracks and breaks up into enormous blocks of ice called **seracs**.

lateral moraine

front of glacier

The mixture of morainal materials that cover the ground is called **till**.

The **terminal moraine** marks the maximum advance of the glacier.

Glacial Erosion

How glaciers transform the landscape

Glaciers are much less prominent today than they were thousands of years ago. When the planet's climate was colder — during periods called ice ages — they covered vast stretches of land. During each of Earth's ice ages, the passage of glaciers left an indelible mark on the landscape. Even today, these rivers of ice are shaping mountains and carving out valleys, creating new topographic shapes.

N

S

TRANSFORMATION OF THE LANDSCAPE BY GLACIERS

BEFORE
The landscape is composed of a V-shaped valley and rounded hills.

During the Pleistocene **ice age**, which ended about ten thousand years ago, ice covered almost 30 percent of Earth's surface, including almost half of Europe and North America.

DURING
The glacier advances into the valley, amassing great quantities of rocks and debris that scrape the sides and bottom of the valley.

AFTER
Once the glacier has passed, the landscape is considerably transformed: the retreating glacier leaves behind a much wider valley and a series of new relief features.

The glacier has created a U-shaped **glacial trough**.

arete

cirque

peak

A side glacier has carved out a **hanging valley**.

Glaciers may carry huge rocks several feet (several m) high: **erratic blocks**.

Drumlins are oval hills whose long sides are parallel to the direction of a glacier's advance.

A **kettle** is a depression in the ground formed when a block of ice melts.

Meltwater held back by moraines forms a **morainal lake**.

Icebergs

Glaciers adrift

In cold regions, glaciers advance as far as the sea without melting. The force of waves and tides then fragments the front of the glacier into gigantic blocks of ice, called icebergs, that float out to sea; only a small part of an iceberg is above water. Propelled by winds and ocean currents, icebergs travel thousands of miles (thousands of km), sometimes drifting as far as the tropics before melting in the ocean under the combined action of waves, salt, and the Sun's rays.

INLAND ICES

The vast continental glaciers that cover almost all of Greenland and Antarctica are called inland ices. These thick layers of ice move very slowly from the center of the land toward the periphery, where they are broken into icebergs in the ocean.

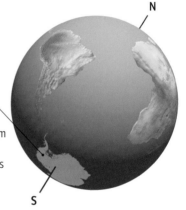

N

The **Greenland inland ice**, an average of .9 mile (1.5 km) thick, covers 660,000 square miles (1.7 million sq km), or 80 percent of the island. Every year, this immense icecap produces 10,000–50,000 icebergs with an average area of .6 square mile (1.6 sq km) and a height of 975 feet (300 m). Some drift as far as the tropical waters near Bermuda.

Greenland inland ice

S

N

Antarctic inland ice

Covering 5.4 million square miles (14 million sq km), with a maximum thickness of 2.7 miles (4.3 km), the **Antarctic inland ice** contains 91 percent of the volume of ice in the world. This huge mass presses the continent down to several thousand feet (several thousand m) below sea level. Each year, the ice sheet produces almost 100,000 icebergs that are usually ten times as big as those from the Arctic.

S

VARIOUS ICEBERG SHAPES

Icebergs are named according to the shape they have above their waterline. The most common are tabular icebergs — large plates that detach from the Antarctic inland ice in great numbers.

tabular iceberg   **dome-shaped iceberg**   **drydocked iceberg**

pinnacled iceberg   **blocky iceberg**   **wedged iceberg**

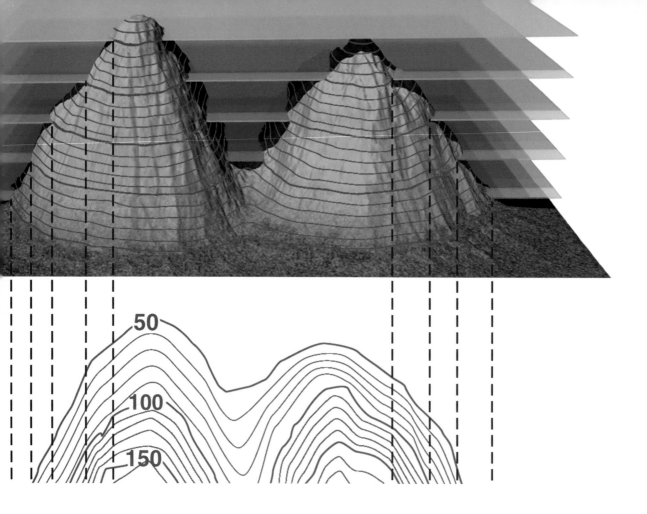

Consulting a world map and finding our way using a city map seem totally natural to us. Yet, the transposition of reality onto paper raises a number of questions. How do we represent the location of a specific site? How can we find out the topography of an inaccessible region? How do we show the altitude of a city? With the latest remote-sensing techniques and systems of graphic conventions, modern cartography gives a very accurate image of our environment in all of its physical and human-made complexity.

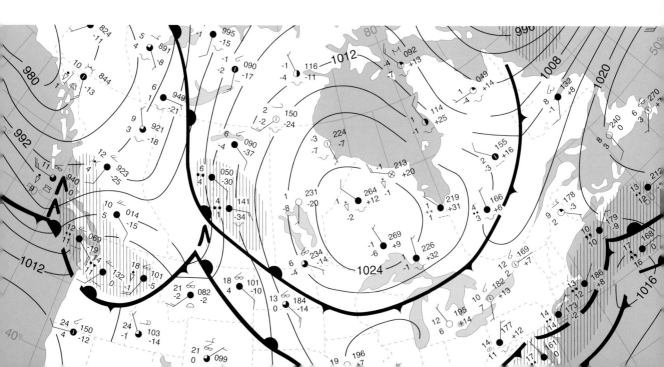

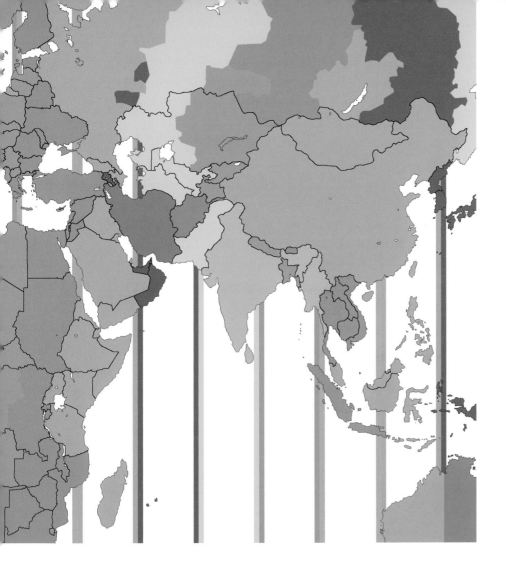

Representations of Earth

Terrestrial Coordinates

Locating ourselves on Earth

Geographers have designed a system of spherical coordinates that allow them to locate any point on Earth using the intersections of imaginary lines parallel to the plane of the equator (latitude) with those parallel to a prime meridian, usually the Greenwich meridian (longitude). The surface of Earth can thus be imagined as being divided into a grid by east–west lines (the parallels) and north–south lines (the meridians).

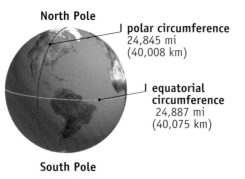

North Pole

polar circumference
24,845 mi
(40,008 km)

equatorial
circumference
24,887 mi
(40,075 km)

South Pole

A SPHERICAL PLANET

Even though it is slightly flatter at the poles, Earth is almost perfectly spherical. Its polar and equatorial circumferences are therefore nearly identical.

NORTH AND SOUTH

The equator, the parallel located exactly halfway between the poles, divides Earth into two parts: the Northern Hemisphere and the Southern Hemisphere.

NORTHERN HEMISPHERE

Atlantic Ocean
North America
Pacific Ocean
North Pole
Asia
Europe

The **Tropic of Cancer**, located at 23°26′ north latitude, is one of the five main parallels. The Sun is directly over it on June 21, the summer solstice.

The **Tropic of Capricorn** is located at 23°26′ south latitude. On the winter solstice, December 21, the Sun is directly over this parallel.

EAST AND WEST

The prime meridian, an imaginary line passing through Greenwich, England, also separates the planet into two parts: the Eastern Hemisphere and the Western Hemisphere.

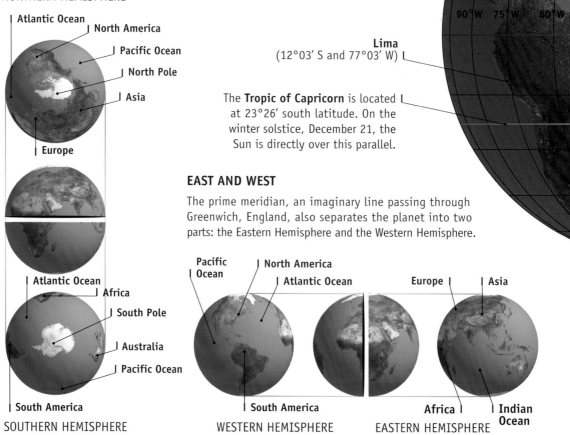

Montreal
(45°30′ N and 73°34′ W)

meridian

90°W   75°W   60°W

Lima
(12°03′ S and 77°03′ W)

Atlantic Ocean
Africa
South Pole
Australia
Pacific Ocean
South America
SOUTHERN HEMISPHERE

Pacific
Ocean
North America
Atlantic Ocean
South America
WESTERN HEMISPHERE

Europe
Asia
Africa
Indian
Ocean
EASTERN HEMISPHERE

THE MERIDIANS AND THE PARALLELS

The **meridians** are imaginary lines converging at the poles and linking all points on Earth with the same longitude. The prime meridian (0°) serves as a reference point for calculating longitudes, ranging from 180°W to 180°E.

The **parallels** are imaginary lines parallel to the equator and linking all points with the same latitude. The equator, located at latitude 0°, is the reference point for calculating latitudes, which range from 90°N (at the North Pole) to 90°S (at the South Pole).

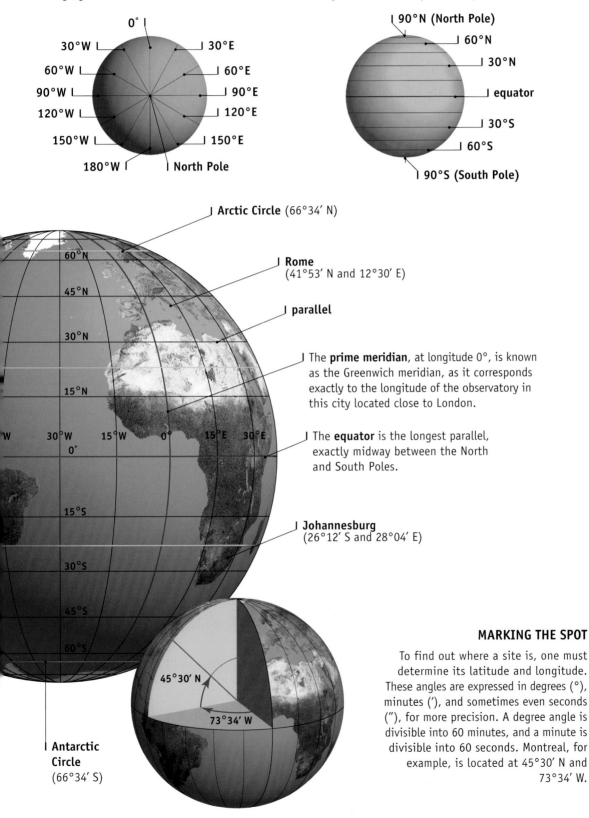

0°
30°W   30°E
60°W   60°E
90°W   90°E
120°W   120°E
150°W   150°E
180°W   North Pole

90°N (North Pole)
60°N
30°N
equator
30°S
60°S
90°S (South Pole)

Arctic Circle (66°34′ N)

60°N

Rome
(41°53′ N and 12°30′ E)

45°N

parallel

30°N

The **prime meridian**, at longitude 0°, is known as the Greenwich meridian, as it corresponds exactly to the longitude of the observatory in this city located close to London.

15°N

W   30°W   15°W   0°   15°E   30°E
0°

The **equator** is the longest parallel, exactly midway between the North and South Poles.

15°S

Johannesburg
(26°12′ S and 28°04′ E)

30°S

45°S

60°S

45°30′ N

73°34′ W

Antarctic Circle
(66°34′ S)

MARKING THE SPOT

To find out where a site is, one must determine its latitude and longitude. These angles are expressed in degrees (°), minutes (′), and sometimes even seconds (″), for more precision. A degree angle is divisible into 60 minutes, and a minute is divisible into 60 seconds. Montreal, for example, is located at 45°30′ N and 73°34′ W.

Cartographic Projection

Representing Earth on a flat surface

Although the curvature of Earth is barely perceptible when a small area is being portrayed, it becomes obvious when a continent is being represented and even more so when the entire planet is being represented. To transpose the surface of Earth onto a flat map, a projection system must be used — a correspondence between reality (in three dimensions) and its representation (in two dimensions).

There are a number of systems, but all of them involve distortion of areas, angles, or distances. The choice of a cartographic projection therefore always results in a compromise that is acceptable for the use to which it will be put.

CYLINDRICAL PROJECTION

When Earth's surface is projected onto a cylinder, the meridians and parallels are represented on the resulting map as straight lines that cross each other at right angles. The equatorial zone is not very distorted, but the polar regions appear rather distorted in the east–west direction.

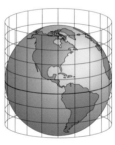

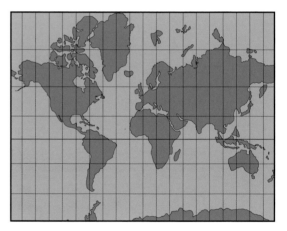

Invented in 1569 by the Dutch geographer Gerard Mercator, the **Mercator projection** compensates for the east–west distortion with an equivalent south–north distortion of the polar regions. Because of this, the Mercator projection preserves the right angles between the parallels and meridians, and it is therefore still one of the most frequently used systems for navigation. However, the correction causes some areas to appear larger, especially closer to the poles.

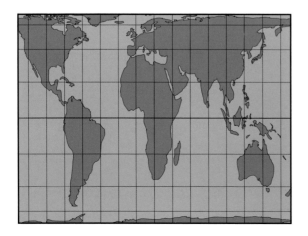

The **Peters projection** cuts the sphere at the 45°N and 45°S parallels. The distortion in distances is thus distributed at the equator and the poles, while the latitudes in the middle are relatively undistorted. This projection system preserves the angles and the areas.

AZIMUTHAL PROJECTION

An azimuthal (or planar) projection is produced on a plane placed so that it is tangential to one point on the planet's surface. The map obtained is circular in shape and represents only one hemisphere. Because the distortion of shapes increases with distance from the tangent point, this type of projection is used mainly to portray polar regions.

If the **tangent point** is a pole, the meridians show as straight lines and the parallels as concentric circles.

CONICAL PROJECTION

A conical projection is obtained by projecting the surface of Earth onto a cone that is in contact with a parallel. On the resulting fan-shaped map, distortions become greater on either side of the contact zone. This projection system, which can portray only part of the planet, is frequently used to produce maps of regions in the middle latitudes.

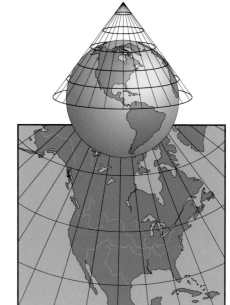

MIXED PROJECTION

Using computers, modern cartographers combine a number of projection types to produce world maps of different shapes and views.

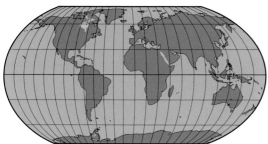

The **Robinson projection** is not really a cylindrical projection, since the meridians other than the prime meridian are not straight lines. Maps produced with this system preserve neither the angles, the areas, nor the distances, but they offer an interesting compromise among these three constraints.

Goode's projection, which combines two projection methods, is called interrupted when the map obtained is not continuous. The interruptions, which do not leave out any part of the planet, are usually placed in the middle of oceans, and the continents are portrayed with very little distortion.

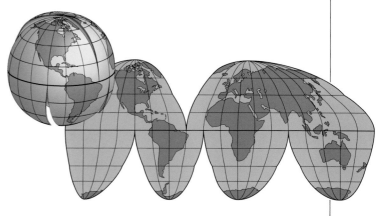

Cartography

Making the world flat

The purpose of a geographic map is to transmit information about natural and human-made features on a part of Earth's surface. A cartographer's job is to create a document that is faithful to the topology of the terrain, on which he or she places graphic symbols that highlight certain characteristics. Making a map is the result of a great deal of time spent collecting, researching, and coding information.

A TERRITORY CUT INTO TRIANGLES

The first step in making a map is to precisely determine a number of points in the region being portrayed: this is called a survey. Measurements of the terrain are made using a procedure called triangulation. After precisely determining the distance between two points, a third point is chosen and the angles it forms with the base of the triangle are measured. Trigonometric calculation is used to determine the lengths of the two other sides of the triangle. From point to point, a basic network is built from which the entire territory can be surveyed.

A **geodetic point** is a point in the territory whose coordinates have been precisely measured.

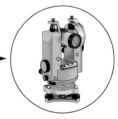

A **theodolite** is used to measure angles precisely.

LEVELING

The most accurate way to determine the altitude of a point in the geodetic network is called direct leveling.
It consists of comparing two graduated level rods, one placed at the point to be measured (B), the other at a nearby point the altitude of which is already known (A). An optical level placed at an equal distance between the two level rods determines the spot grade (difference in altitude) between the two points. This operation is performed from point to point over the entire territory starting from base level (sea level).

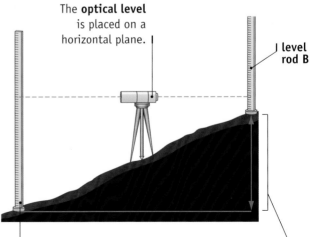

The **optical level** is placed on a horizontal plane.

level rod B

level rod A

The **spot grade** is obtained by subtracting the value of rod level B from that of rod level A.

AERIAL PHOTOGRAPHY

The geodetic network is a basic framework to which many other data must be added. Since the mid-twentieth century, surveys of these elements have usually been done with aerial photography. An airplane flies at a constant altitude, speed, and direction over the territory to be surveyed and takes pictures at regular intervals, with each image overlapping part of the preceding one. Using the overlapping parts of two successive photographs, the cartographer can view the territory in three dimensions with a stereoscope.

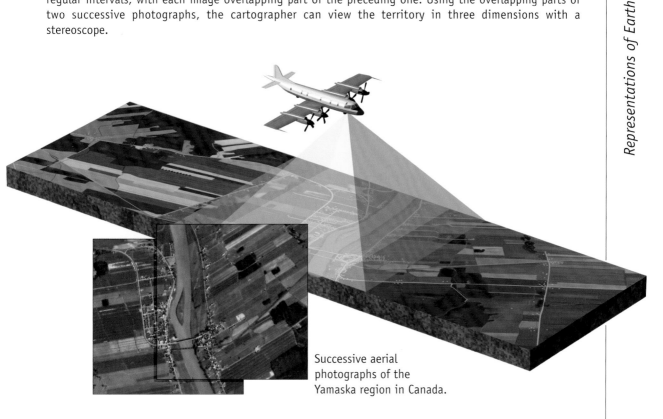

Successive aerial
photographs of the
Yamaska region in Canada.

THE BASE MAP

A field completion survey — a supplementary study of the territory — provides data that aerial photography cannot supply: place names, types of roads, elements hidden by vegetation, and so on. All of the information obtained is then used to draw a very accurate map of the territory, generally at a scale of 1/20,000. This base map will be used as a reference for the making of all sorts of derived maps.

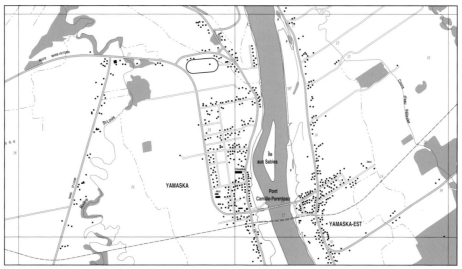

Base map (1/20,000) of the Yamaska region in Canada.

Cartographic Conventions

Tools for reading a map

To represent reality, the cartographer must translate data that have been gathered into comprehensible graphic elements. This complex operation is based on conventional symbols, defined in the map legend, that the reader must learn to decode. Aside from graphic symbols (pictograms, colors, grids, typography), maps use other conventions, such as scale, orientation, and generalization.

SCALES

The distances measured on a map are proportional to the real distances that they represent. This constant ratio, which is the scale of the map, is expressed either by a fraction or graphically. Each scale has its advantages: a large-scale map shows more detail, while a small-scale map shows a greater area.

The smaller the scale of a map, the more simplified and selected the tracings must be. This adjustment is called generalization. At a scale of 1/1,300,000, 1 cm (.39 inch) on a map represents about 8 miles (13 km) on the ground ❶. At a scale of 1/400,000, 1 cm (.39 inch) on a map represents about 2.5 miles (4 km) on the ground ❷. At a scale of 1/130,000, 1 cm (.39 inch) on a map represents about .8 mile (1.3 km) on the ground ❸.

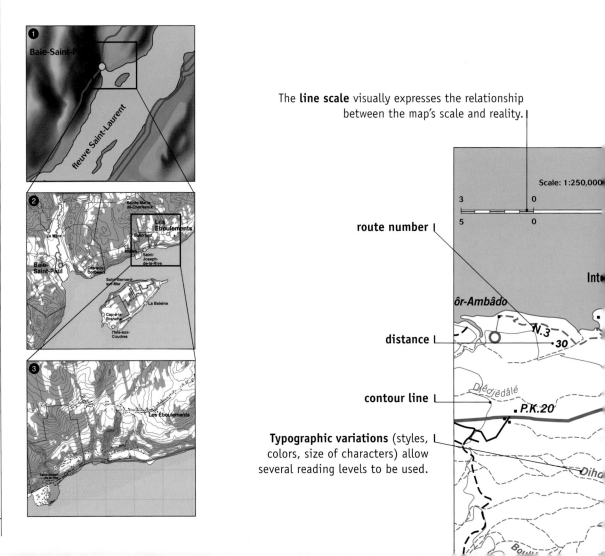

The **line scale** visually expresses the relationship between the map's scale and reality.

Scale: 1:250,000

route number

distance

contour line

Typographic variations (styles, colors, size of characters) allow several reading levels to be used.

HOW TO READ A MAP

Maps of all types use different graphic conventions to express reality. Colors are often used to represent altitudes, create a hierarchy for certain elements (such as roads), and to differentiate adjacent zones. The shape of symbols, whether or not they evoke the reality they represent, can vary widely. Text transmits place names, which may be listed in an index. A hierarchy can be created with typographic variations — for example, by the use of upper-case and lower-case letters. Aside from indicating latitude and longitude, some maps have an alphanumeric grid (composed of numbers and letters) to provide reference points.

The **legend** is the set of operating instructions for a map. It is an inset that provides the reader with the meaning of all the symbols used, such as relief features, roads, size of cities, types of vegetation, and hydrography.

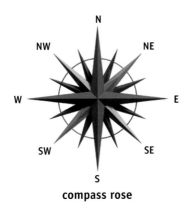

compass rose

Although, by convention, the top of a map usually indicates north, its orientation is often specified, either simply by an arrow pointing north or by a **compass rose** indicating the four cardinal points (north, east, south, west) and the intermediary positions (northeast, southeast, southwest, and northwest).

▬▬▬▬	Paved road
▬ ▬ ▬ ▬	Unpaved road
▬ ▬ ▬	Path
┼┼┼┼	Railway
▨	Urban zone
○ ▪	Village Settlement
ⵣ ⵜ	Mosque Church
⊠	Post office
⊞ ✚	Hospital Dispensary
▱ ✕	School Market
▲ ⚲	Pylon Police station
🏛 ⛽	Hotel Gas station
—x—x—	Edge of regulated zone
▮ ▭	Forest Flood-prone land
⊥⊥⊥⊥⊥	Embankment
⚲ ⛵	Lighthouse Shipwreck
✈	Airport
‑‑‑‑‑‑	Temporary watercourse
●	Water tower

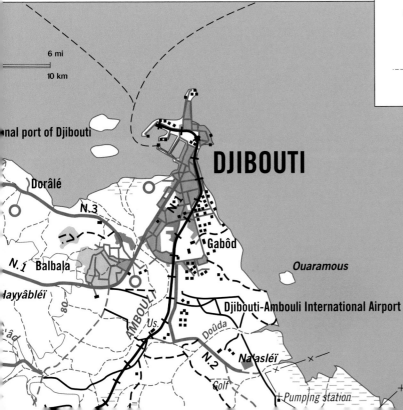

6 mi
10 km

...nal port of Djibouti

Dorâlé

N.3

DJIBOUTI

○

N.1 Balbala

Gabôd

Ouaramous

...ayyâbléï

80

Us.

Djibouti-Ambouli International Airport

AMBOULI

Doûda

N.2

Na'asléï

Golf

✝ Pumping station

Physical and Topographic Maps

The illusion of relief

The goal of physical and topographic maps is to give the most exact image possible of Earth's surface (such as relief features, watercourses, stretches of water, roads, and cities). These maps use various techniques to represent relief features, including contour lines, a color scale, or shading.

CONTOUR LINES

Contour lines are imaginary lines that link all points located at the same altitude. They allow readers to recognize easily different types of relief features: widely spaced lines correspond to an almost flat surface, while lines placed close together illustrate a steep slope. It is thus possible to distinguish hills, cliffs, valleys, plateaus, plains, etc.

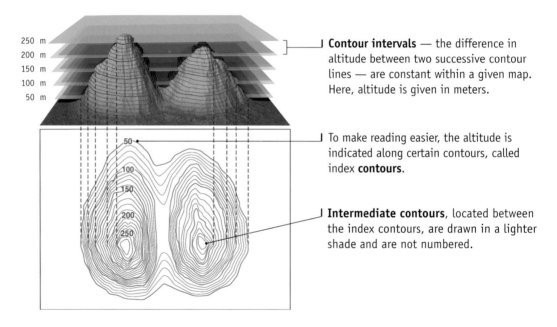

Contour intervals — the difference in altitude between two successive contour lines — are constant within a given map. Here, altitude is given in meters.

To make reading easier, the altitude is indicated along certain contours, called index **contours**.

Intermediate contours, located between the index contours, are drawn in a lighter shade and are not numbered.

THE TOPOGRAPHIC MAP

Drawn on a large scale, the topographic map covers only a small amount of territory. Its extreme precision means that it portrays the relief features of the terrain, using contour lines, and a large number of natural and human-made details, such as vegetation, watercourses, built structures, and roads. It also indicates territorial boundaries and place names.

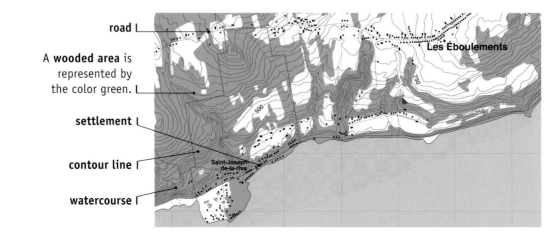

road

A **wooded area** is represented by the color green.

settlement

contour line

watercourse

Les Éboulements

Saint-Joseph-de-la-rive

COLOR SCALES

In smaller-scale physical maps, contour lines are rarely used. They are replaced by areas of color corresponding to altitude levels. The meaning of the colors is given in a legend. On this map, altitude is given in feet.

ALTITUDE (IN FEET)

- \> 3,000
- 2,000–3,000
- 1,000–2,000
- 500–1,000
- 200–500
- 0–200

RELIEF FEATURES IN PROFILE

A cross-section view of an area shows the variation in relief along a straight line scribed onto the map.

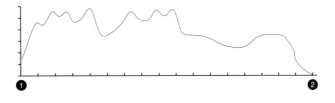

The **light source** is never explicitly given on the map; the orientation of shadows provides an indication.

valley

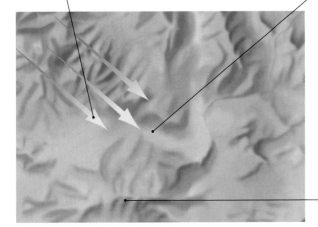

RELIEF SHADING

Relief shading is a graphic technique that gives the illusion of relief. The cartographer simulates the effects of a light source by stumping (lightly shading) the slopes in shadow. This procedure does not give an indication of altitude, but mountainous regions can be easily distinguished from plains and plateaus. Valleys and mountain peaks can also be seen.

arete

Thematic Maps

A variety of applications

Cartography is not limited to showing the physical aspects of a territory. Some maps are capable of presenting a wide variety of quantitative or qualitative phenomena, if they can be located geographically. These thematic maps use a topographic map as a background, but they leave out most of the details of that map to highlight a very specific phenomenon using a graphic language. Climate, demographics, natural resources, economics, and even phenomena that vary over time — thematic maps can portray a wide variety of subjects.

THE GRAPHIC LANGUAGE OF THEMATIC MAPS

Even more than topographic maps, thematic maps use a structured graphic language. The visual symbols used to localize a phenomenon portray the type of facility, which may be localized (city), linear (railroad line), or zonal (population density). Variations in size, shape, or color distinguish the various graphic symbols according to quantitative, qualitative, or even hierarchical criteria.

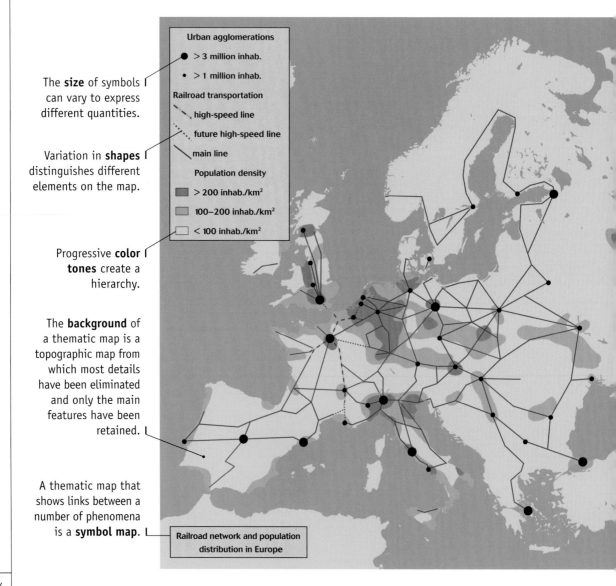

The **size** of symbols can vary to express different quantities.

Variation in **shapes** distinguishes different elements on the map.

Progressive **color tones** create a hierarchy.

The **background** of a thematic map is a topographic map from which most details have been eliminated and only the main features have been retained.

A thematic map that shows links between a number of phenomena is a **symbol map**.

Urban agglomerations
● > 3 million inhab.
• > 1 million inhab.

Railroad transportation
high-speed line
future high-speed line
main line

Population density
> 200 inhab./km²
100–200 inhab./km²
< 100 inhab./km²

Railroad network and population distribution in Europe

HISTORY THROUGH MAPS

Unlike topographic maps, which present the state of a territory at a given moment, thematic maps can express the evolution of phenomena over time through different cartographic techniques.

Map ❶ uses a range of colors to represent the growth of the European Union as new countries join. The gradation of colors (each one corresponding to a year) gives a visual impression of progression through time.

In map ❷, which shows migrations of Gypsies in Europe, the passage of time is represented by a series of arrows linking places where this nomadic people has settled over time. The date when Gypsies arrived in Europe is indicated directly on the map, beside the respective city name.

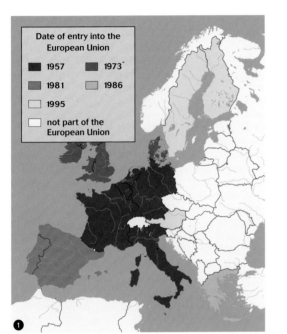

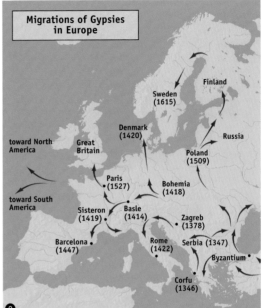

METEOROLOGICAL MAPS

Meteorologists have developed a complex system of graphic signs and conventions that enables them to give a very precise representation of the atmospheric state of a region at a given moment. Meteorological maps generally do not have legends, since this system is subject to very strict international codification.

Atmospheric fronts are shown by thicker lines.

Isobars are lines that join all points with the same atmospheric pressure.

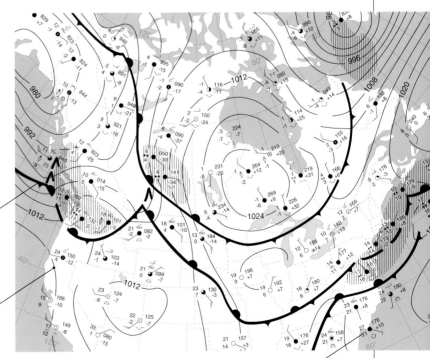

Symbols indicate the type of precipitation and wind strength and direction at each weather station.

Remote Sensing

Observing Earth from on high

Most geological structures and phenomena extend over considerable distances, which makes them impossible to observe on a human scale. Remote sensing — acquisition of information from a distance — calls on different imaging techniques (photography, radar, sonar) that allow us to view the planet's surface from a distance so that we can better examine it. The data gathered have applications in a great number of disciplines, from cartography to agriculture.

AERIAL PHOTOGRAPHY

Photography, which captures wavelengths in the visible spectrum, is the simplest and oldest remote-sensing system. The first aerial photographs were taken from a balloon by Frenchman Félix Nadar in 1858.

REMOTE SENSING BY ECHO

Radar and sonar are remote-sensing instruments that use the principle of echoes to detect masses at a distance. In both cases, waves are emitted in a certain frequency, then the part of the radiation that the object reflects is captured and analyzed to determine its distance and position. The data received are used to produce automatically an image of the zone observed.

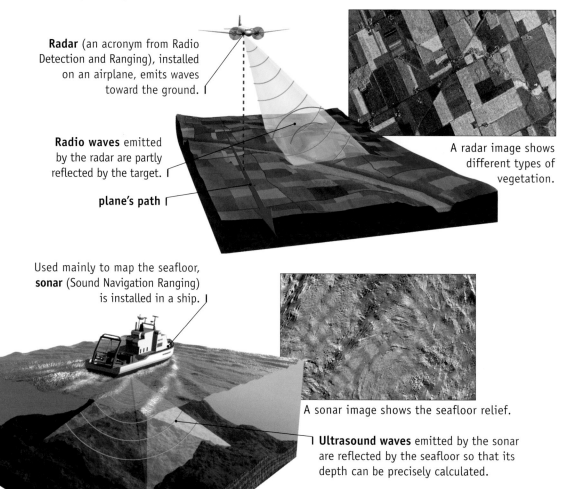

Radar (an acronym from Radio Detection and Ranging), installed on an airplane, emits waves toward the ground.

Radio waves emitted by the radar are partly reflected by the target.

plane's path

A radar image shows different types of vegetation.

Used mainly to map the seafloor, **sonar** (Sound Navigation Ranging) is installed in a ship.

A sonar image shows the seafloor relief.

Ultrasound waves emitted by the sonar are reflected by the seafloor so that its depth can be precisely calculated.

PASSIVE AND ACTIVE SENSORS

Satellites that observe Earth's surface also use radar. In the classic remote-sensing process, the Sun's natural radiation ❶, partially reflected ❷ by most surfaces, is collected by a passive sensor ❸. But atmospheric conditions sometimes prevent illumination of the target by the Sun. Then, an active sensor ❹, capable of emitting electromagnetic radiation ❺ in different frequencies and capturing the part reflected from the ground ❻, is used. In both cases, the sensor sends ❼ the raw data to a ground station ❽ for analysis and interpretation.

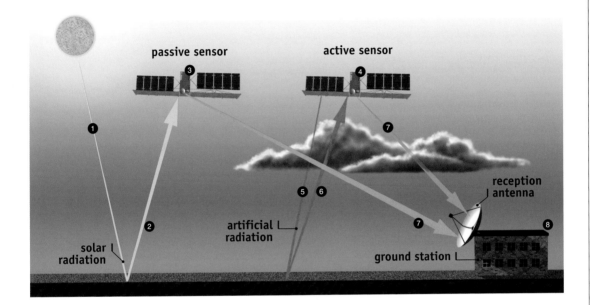

SPECTRAL SIGNATURE

Each object emits and reflects electromagnetic radiation according to its physical properties. By measuring this radiation, the object's reflectance — the relationship between the radiation it has received and reflected in a given wavelength — is determined. The spectral behavior of an object is its signature.

DIFFERENTIATING SURFACES

The spectral signature of objects is sometimes the only way of distinguishing them when they are observed from space. While healthy vegetation looks blue in the image below when sensed in the infrared spectrum, diseased trees show up in red.

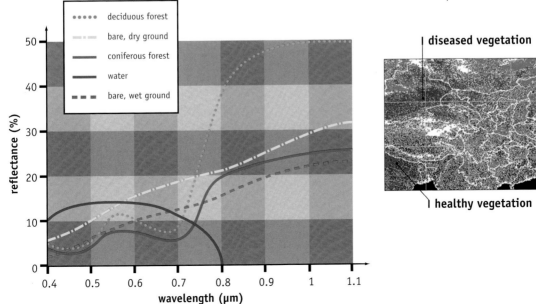

diseased vegetation

healthy vegetation

Satellites and Shuttles

Eyes in space

Until recently, we did not have very detailed maps of the entire planet. Some regions were difficult to access and climatic conditions sometimes kept airplanes from flying or their equipment from photographing the ground. The use of radar by remote-sensing satellites now has made it possible to make complete and precise maps of Earth's surface.

Observation with a **standard beam** ❶ shows the major geological formations of the island of Maui, in the Hawaiian archipelago.

A **fine-resolution beam** ❷ shows the airport runways on the island.

RADARSAT STUDIES EARTH

The Canadian satellite *Radarsat 1*, launched in 1995, observes environmental changes and the use of Earth's resources. Because the satellite has a polar orbit and the planet rotates to the east, each pass of *Radarsat* is shifted to the west in relation to the previous one. This enables it to cover all of the planet's surface.

Radarsat's powerful synthetic aperture radar (SAR) is able to collect images of Earth both day and night and in all climatic conditions. It can direct several types of beams along a 300-foot- (500-km-) wide corridor at resolutions of between 26 feet and 39 feet (8 m and 100 m) and at angles of incidence from 20° to 49°.

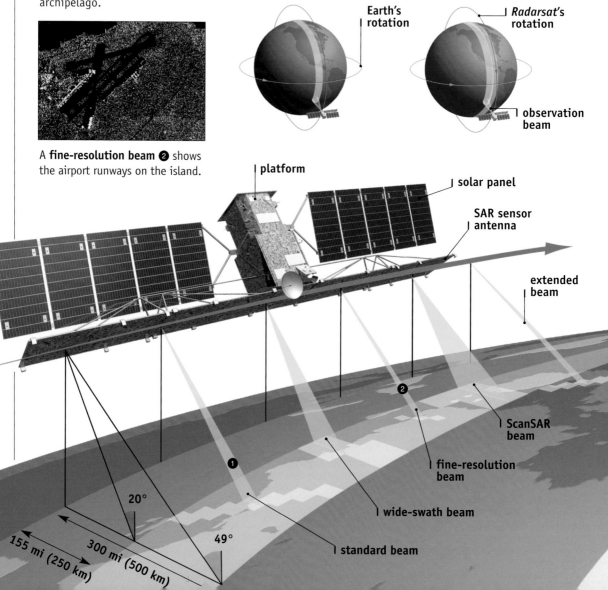

Earth's rotation

Radarsat's rotation

observation beam

platform

solar panel

SAR sensor antenna

extended beam

ScanSAR beam

fine-resolution beam

wide-swath beam

standard beam

20°

49°

155 mi (250 km)

300 mi (500 km)

THE SRTM MISSION

In February 2000, NASA conducted the most ambitious Earth-mapping mission yet, called STRM (Shuttle Radar Topography Mission). The SRTM system, installed on the *Endeavor* Space Shuttle, observed all landmasses located between parallels 60° North and 56° South, where 95 percent of the world's population lives. The group of images taken by the SRTM during its ten-day flight make up the most complete and precise topographic map of Earth ever made.

HOW THE SRTM MAPS EARTH

The SRTM's main antenna emits radar waves in the C-band toward the zone to be mapped. How the zone reflects the radiation depends on the nature of its surface and its relief. The combination of signals collected by the SRTM's two antennas (main and external) make it possible to generate a three-dimensional image of the zone.

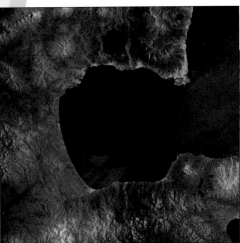

The SRTM **mast**, 195 feet (60 m) long, is the longest rigid structure ever deployed in orbit aside from the International Space Station.

external antenna

C-band rays cover a swath (corridor) of 140 miles (225 km).

X-band rays, limited to a swath of 30 miles (50 km), supply finer-resolution images.

The **main antenna** emits 1,500 radar pulses toward Earth per second.

THE APPLICATIONS

Scientists will use the data from the SRTM to conduct geological, hydrological, and geophysical studies. Civil applications range from land-use management to installation of cellular-telephone networks. The U.S. military will use these extremely accurate topographic maps for personnel training, logistical planning, and missile-guidance systems.

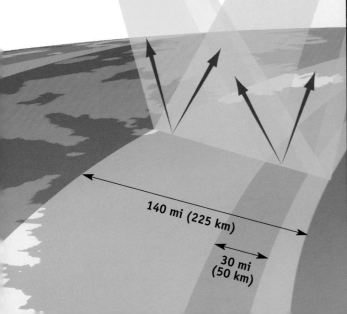

140 mi (225 km)

30 mi (50 km)

The island of Hokkaido, in Japan. Altitude is represented by different colors, from blue for the lowest areas to white for the highest areas.

Time Zones

The world in 24 hours

Solar time, which is calculated according to the Sun's position in the sky, is different at each meridian; it therefore cannot be used as a common reference. The development of transportation and communications in the nineteenth century led different countries to institute an international system that made it easy to establish the time at every point on the planet. In 1883, Earth's surface was divided into twenty-four time zones, imaginary zones spread uniformly around the globe. Each of these zones has a single standard time, determined in relation to the standard time in the Greenwich (England) time zone.

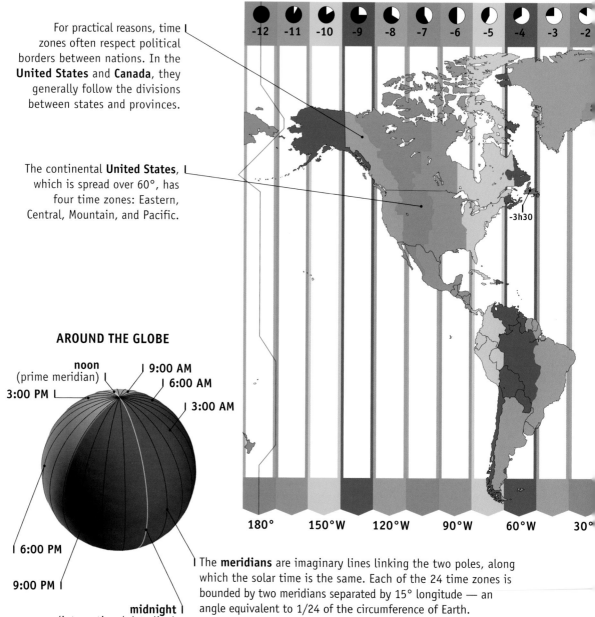

For practical reasons, time zones often respect political borders between nations. In the **United States** and **Canada**, they generally follow the divisions between states and provinces.

The continental **United States**, which is spread over 60°, has four time zones: Eastern, Central, Mountain, and Pacific.

-3h30

AROUND THE GLOBE

noon
(prime meridian)

9:00 AM

6:00 AM

3:00 PM

3:00 AM

6:00 PM

9:00 PM

midnight
(international date line)

-12 -11 -10 -9 -8 -7 -6 -5 -4 -3 -2

180°   150°W   120°W   90°W   60°W   30°

The **meridians** are imaginary lines linking the two poles, along which the solar time is the same. Each of the 24 time zones is bounded by two meridians separated by 15° longitude — an angle equivalent to 1/24 of the circumference of Earth.

GREENWICH TIME

Britain's supremacy in the nineteenth century determined the choice of the Greenwich meridian, the site of an old observatory (see photo right), as the universal time reference. The civil time at Greenwich, called Universal Time (UT), is the reference point for the entire planet. To obtain the legal time for a location, add or subtract from UT the number of hours equivalent to the number of time zones it is away from Greenwich time.

The Greenwich meridian is called the **prime meridian**, since it is conventionally used as the reference point for the longitudinal division of the planet.

The territory of the **Russian Federation** is divided into ten time zones.

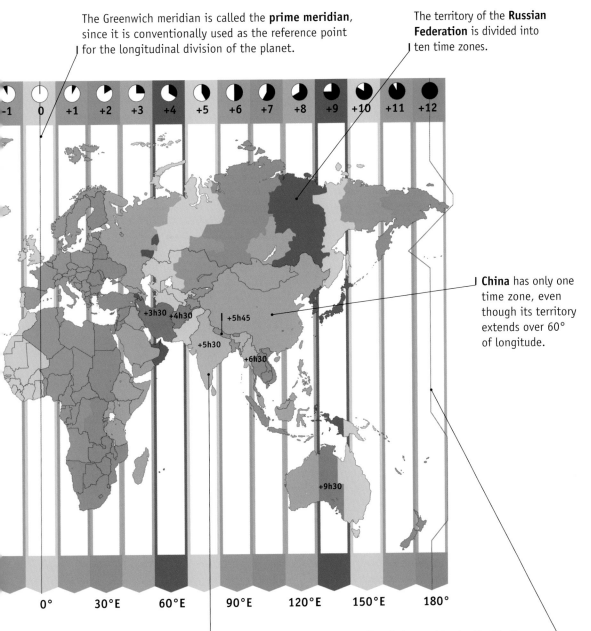

China has only one time zone, even though its territory extends over 60° of longitude.

Some countries, such as **India**, have chosen a legal time shifted by one half-hour from neighboring time zones.

The **international date line** is located in the Pacific Ocean at longitude 180° — that is, directly opposite the Greenwich meridian. When we cross this line, we go forward or backward by one day, depending on whether we are traveling east or west. The line deviates in several places to avoid having countries or island groups divided into two different dates.

Unlike the innumerable small islands on the planet, many of which were made by local volcanic action, the seven continents are attached to vast tectonic masses, the continental plates. From the Andes Cordillera to the Sahara Desert, from the Great Barrier Reef to the Yellow River, from an Antarctic ice sheet to the crater on Mount Vesuvius, the great diversity of our planet and its relief features are explored in this section.

The Continents

The Configuration of the Continents

The planet's landmasses

The continents are vast stretches of land surrounded by water, and they represent about one-third of the planet's surface. Each one has very different characteristics (such as area, relief features, and inland seas) — and even different boundaries, depending on who is measuring them. Generally, geographers consider only the part of the landmass that is not underwater, while geologists include the coastal margins: the continental shelves that extend under the sea and end with steep slopes beyond which the oceanic basins start.

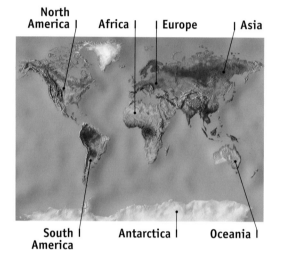

North America | Africa | | Europe | | Asia

South America | Antarctica | Oceania |

THE SEVEN CONTINENTS

Today, we divide Earth's landmasses into seven continents: Europe, Asia, Africa, North America, South America, Oceania, and Antarctica. For historical and ethnological reasons, geographers have divided Europe and Asia, which in reality form one large continent (Eurasia).

In addition, some neighboring islands have sometimes been arbitrarily classified as parts of continents.

THE STRUCTURE OF THE CONTINENTS

Over time, many factors (such as plate tectonics, volcanism, erosion, or sedimentation) have transformed the relief features of Earth and its continents. In spite of their differences, the continents all have older (more stable) parts, younger (more active) parts, and a similar underlying structure. Each rests on a platform of bedrock dating from the Precambrian Eon, around which are sedimentary basins and old mountain ranges (rounded peaks, located near the shield) or recent (scarped, near the coasts).

The **shield** (or platform) contains the oldest geologic layers and is generally located in the interior of continents.

The **sedimentary basins**, located in adjoining zones, are depressions in which sediments have accumulated.

Mountain chains surround the continental system and are found near the shield or bordering the coasts.

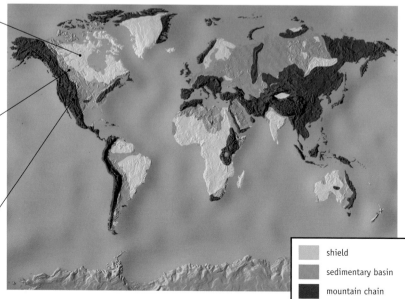

shield

sedimentary basin

mountain chain

Antarctica

The ends of Earth

Antarctica is the only uninhabited continent, yet it is larger than Europe and Australia. With an area of 5.5 million square miles (14 million sq km), 98 percent of its land is covered with an icecap up to 13,000 feet (4,000 m) thick. This layer of ice contains 90 percent of the planet's freshwater reserves (12 million square miles [30 million sq km]). The few rocky outcroppings are the only ice-free spaces.

ANTARCTICA IN FIGURES	
total area	5,500,000 sq mi (14,200,000 sq km)
highest point	Vinson Massif 16,900 ft (5,140 m)

Transantarctic Mountains

Ross Ice Shelf

Most of **West Antarctica** consists of sedimentary basins lying below sea level, forming many epicontinental islands connected by the ice sheet. Dominated by mountain chains, it is much smaller than East Antarctica and is shaped somewhat like a peninsula.

East Antarctica, which forms the continent's platform, is the older and larger part.

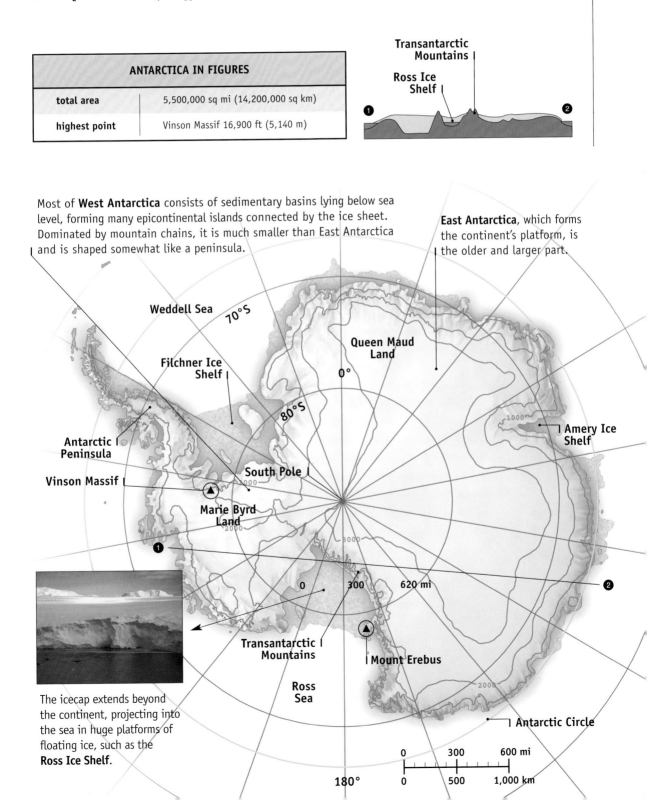

Weddell Sea
70°S
Filchner Ice Shelf
Queen Maud Land
0°
80°S
Amery Ice Shelf
Antarctic Peninsula
Vinson Massif
South Pole
Marie Byrd Land
620 mi
300
0
Transantarctic Mountains
Mount Erebus
Ross Sea
Antarctic Circle

The icecap extends beyond the continent, projecting into the sea in huge platforms of floating ice, such as the **Ross Ice Shelf**.

| 0 | 300 | 600 mi |
| 0 | 500 | 1,000 km |

180°

North America

A continent of wide-open spaces

North America, with 16 percent of the planet's total landmass, is bounded by the Pacific, Atlantic, and Arctic oceans. The oldest part of the continent, the Canadian Shield, borders Hudson Bay. Around the shield, major drainage basins (the St. Lawrence and the Great Lakes, the Mississippi, and the Mackenzie) stretch across the North American platform.

While the Appalachian, an old and eroded mountain range, are the main relief feature of the east side of the continent, the west side is dominated by a high mountain belt (the Rockies and the Sierra Madre) that runs parallel to the Pacific coast from Alaska to Mexico. The belt extends into the isthmus of Central America, which, with the string of islands forming the Lesser and Greater Antilles, borders the Caribbean Sea.

The Western Cordillera includes the Rocky Mountains, to the north, and the Sierra Madre, to the south. **Mount McKinley**, in Alaska, is the highest mountain in North America.

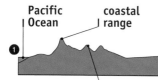

Death Valley in California, a deep rift valley 280 feet (86 m) below sea level, is an unusally arid zone.

Pacific Ocean | coastal range | Atlantic Ocean

❶ ❷

Rocky Mountains | Appalachians

NORTH AMERICA IN FIGURES	
total area	9,354,935 mi² (24,235,583 km²)
highest point	Mount McKinley 20,131 ft (6,194 m)
lowest point	Death Valley -280 ft (-86 m)
longest river	Mississippi-Missouri 4,080 mi (5,970 km)
largest lake	Superior 31,690 mi² (82,100 km²)
largest island	Greenland 839,550 mi² (2,175,000 km²)

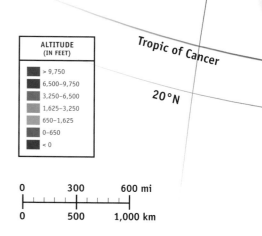

80°N
160°W

Bering Strait

60°N

Gulf of Alaska

Vancouver Island

40°N

❶

Pacific Ocean

Tropic of Cancer

20°N

ALTITUDE (IN FEET)	
	> 9,750
	6,500–9,750
	3,250–6,500
	1,625–3,250
	650–1,625
	0–650
	< 0

0   300   600 mi

0   500   1,000 km

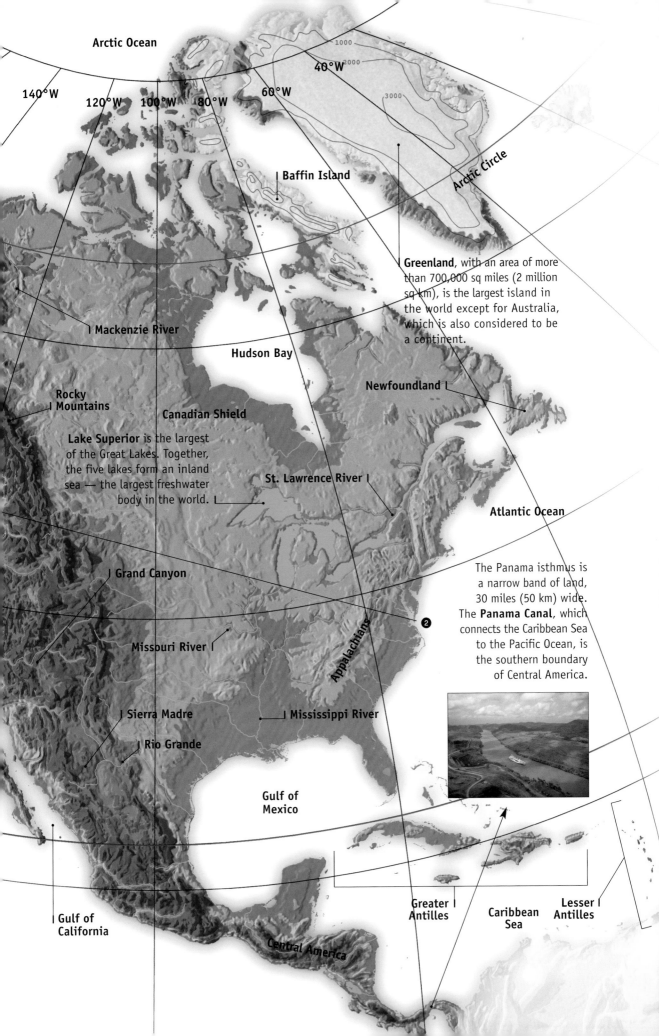

Arctic Ocean

1000
2000
3000

40°W

60°W

140°W

120°W

100°W

80°W

Baffin Island

Arctic Circle

Greenland, with an area of more than 700,000 sq miles (2 million sq km), is the largest island in the world except for Australia, which is also considered to be a continent.

Mackenzie River

Hudson Bay

Newfoundland

Rocky Mountains

Canadian Shield

Lake Superior is the largest of the Great Lakes. Together, the five lakes form an inland sea — the largest freshwater body in the world.

St. Lawrence River

Atlantic Ocean

Grand Canyon

Appalachians

❷

The Panama isthmus is a narrow band of land, 30 miles (50 km) wide. The **Panama Canal**, which connects the Caribbean Sea to the Pacific Ocean, is the southern boundary of Central America.

Missouri River

Sierra Madre

Mississippi River

Rio Grande

Gulf of Mexico

Gulf of California

Greater Antilles

Caribbean Sea

Lesser Antilles

Central America

South America

A continent of contrasts

South America accounts for 12 percent of the planet's landmass. Bounded by the Pacific and Atlantic Oceans, it has relief features similar to those of North America. The eastern part of the continent sits on an old platform, represented by the Guiana Highlands in the north, the Brazilian Highlands in the center, and Patagonia in the south. These plateaus are separated by depressions irrigated by major rivers: the Orinoco, the Amazon, and the Paraná. The great mountain ranges are on the west coast: the Andes Cordillera stretches north to south from Venezuela to southern Chile, where the very jagged coastline bears testimony to former glaciation. From the high peaks of the Andes to the chilly regions of Patagonia, via the equatorial plains of Amazonia, South America is truly a land of contrasts.

equator

10°S

The **Andes Cordillera** represents the highest mountain range on the planet, after the Himalayas. Stretching for almost 5,000 miles (8,000 km), it is the longest range in the world. Almost fifty of its peaks have an altitude of more than 19,500 feet (6,000 m).

20°S

Tropic of Capricorn

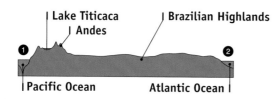

| Lake Titicaca | Brazilian Highlands
| Andes
Pacific Ocean   Atlantic Ocean

30°S

Pacific Ocean

40°S

SOUTH AMERICA IN FIGURES	
total area	6,876,000 mi² (17,814,000 km²)
highest point	Aconcagua 22,620 ft (6,960 m)
lowest point	Valdés Peninsula -130 ft (-40 m)
longest river	Amazon 4,080 mi (6,570 km)
largest lake	Titicaca 3,200 mi² (8,300 km²)
highest waterfall	Angel Falls 3,182 ft (979 m)

ALTITUDE (IN FEET)

■	> 9,750
■	6,500-9,750
■	3,250-6,500
■	1,625-3,250
■	650-1,625
■	0-650
■	< 0

0   300   600 mi

0   500   1,000 km

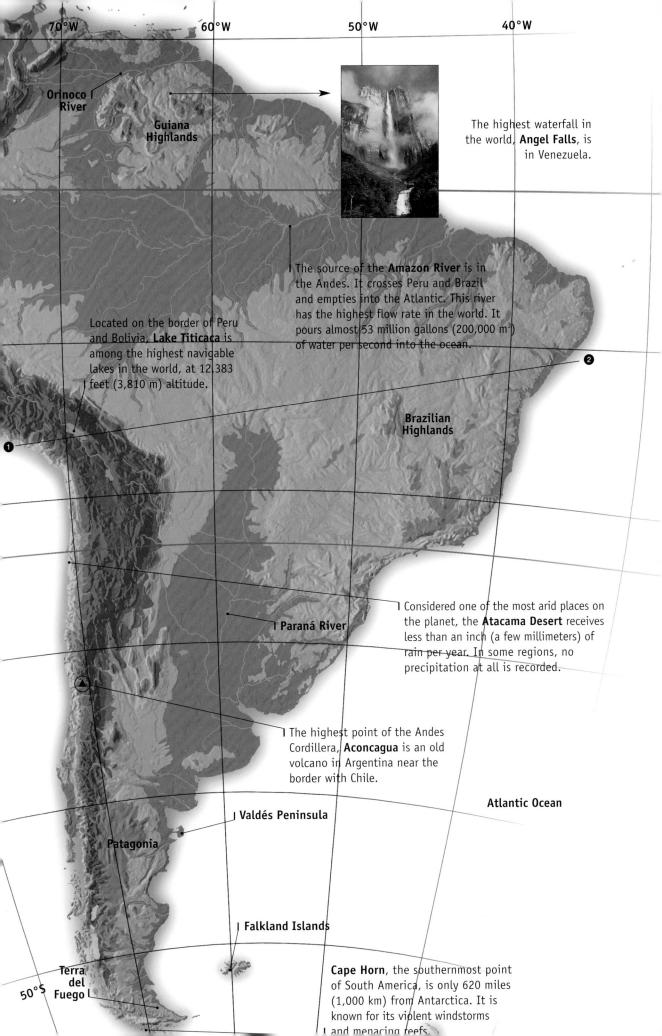

70°W 60°W 50°W 40°W

Orinoco River

Guiana Highlands

The highest waterfall in the world, **Angel Falls**, is in Venezuela.

The source of the **Amazon River** is in the Andes. It crosses Peru and Brazil and empties into the Atlantic. This river has the highest flow rate in the world. It pours almost 53 million gallons (200,000 m³) of water per second into the ocean.

Located on the border of Peru and Bolivia, **Lake Titicaca** is among the highest navigable lakes in the world, at 12,383 feet (3,810 m) altitude.

❷

Brazilian Highlands

❶

Considered one of the most arid places on the planet, the **Atacama Desert** receives less than an inch (a few millimeters) of rain per year. In some regions, no precipitation at all is recorded.

Paraná River

The highest point of the Andes Cordillera, **Aconcagua** is an old volcano in Argentina near the border with Chile.

Atlantic Ocean

Valdés Peninsula

Patagonia

Falkland Islands

Terra del Fuego

50°S

Cape Horn, the southernmost point of South America, is only 620 miles (1,000 km) from Antarctica. It is known for its violent windstorms and menacing reefs.

Europe

A peninsula with an irregular coastline

At the western end of the huge Eurasian continent, Europe is relatively small in size (7 percent of the planet's landmass). Its irregular shape is interspersed with seas (Mediterranean Sea, Black Sea, Baltic Sea, North Sea), which contain numerous islands (such as the British Isles, Corsica, Sardinia, and Sicily).

Europe is divided into four major systems: the northwestern highlands, composed of old geological folds and marked by the passage of glaciers; the North European Plains; the old eroded central highlands (the Massif Central, the Urals); and Alpine-Mediterranean Europe, to the south, formed of high mountain ranges (Pyrenees, Alps, and Carpathians).

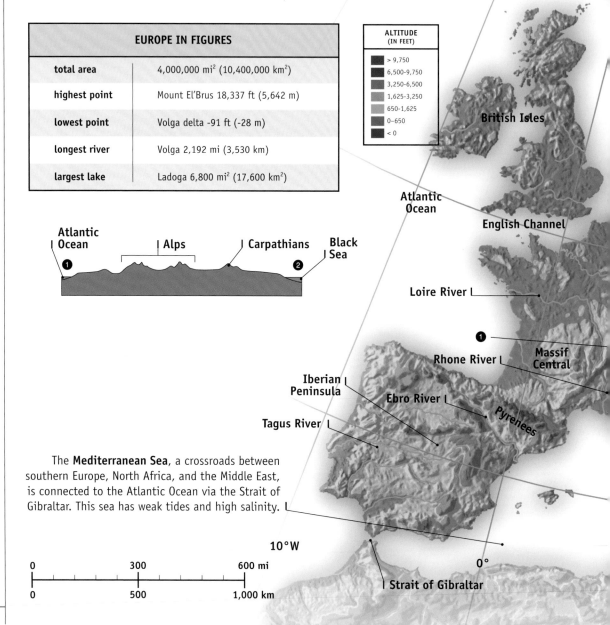

EUROPE IN FIGURES	
total area	4,000,000 mi² (10,400,000 km²)
highest point	Mount El'Brus 18,337 ft (5,642 m)
lowest point	Volga delta -91 ft (-28 m)
longest river	Volga 2,192 mi (3,530 km)
largest lake	Ladoga 6,800 mi² (17,600 km²)

ALTITUDE (IN FEET)

- > 9,750
- 6,500-9,750
- 3,250-6,500
- 1,625-3,250
- 650-1,625
- 0-650
- < 0

Iceland

British Isles

Atlantic Ocean

English Channel

Atlantic Ocean | Alps | Carpathians | Black Sea
❶ ❷

Loire River

❶

Rhone River

Massif Central

Iberian Peninsula

Ebro River

Pyrenees

Tagus River

The **Mediterranean Sea**, a crossroads between southern Europe, North Africa, and the Middle East, is connected to the Atlantic Ocean via the Strait of Gibraltar. This sea has weak tides and high salinity.

10°W

0°

Strait of Gibraltar

| 0 | 300 | 600 mi |
| 0 | 500 | 1,000 km |

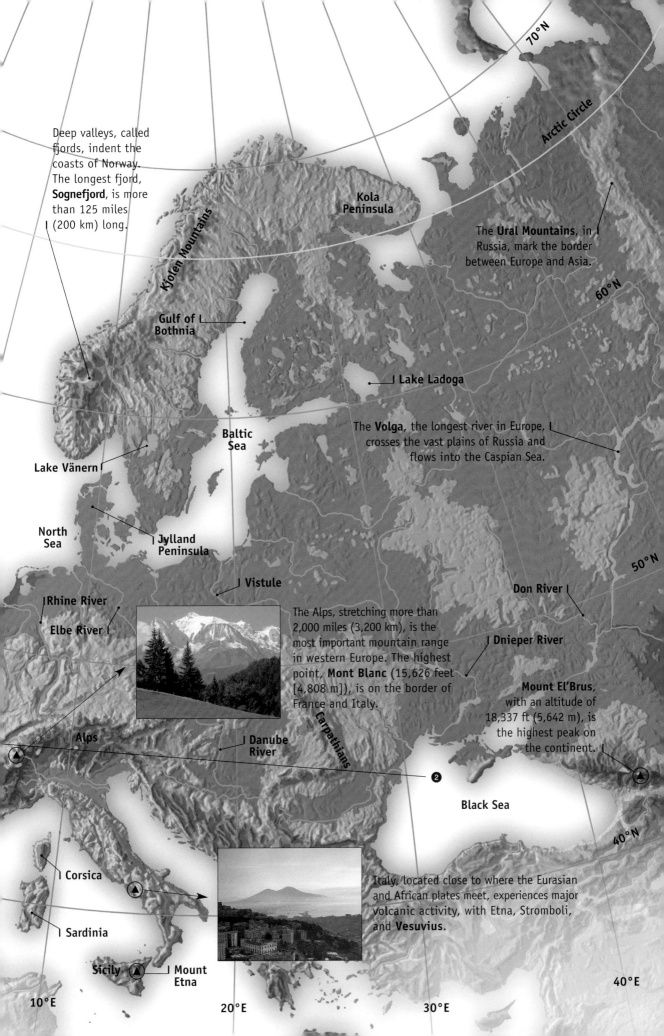

Deep valleys, called fjords, indent the coasts of Norway. The longest fjord, **Sognefjord**, is more than 125 miles (200 km) long.

Kjølen Mountains

Kola Peninsula

The **Ural Mountains**, in Russia, mark the border between Europe and Asia.

70°N

Arctic Circle

60°N

Gulf of Bothnia

Lake Ladoga

Baltic Sea

The **Volga**, the longest river in Europe, crosses the vast plains of Russia and flows into the Caspian Sea.

Lake Vänern

North Sea

Jylland Peninsula

50°N

Vistule

Don River

Rhine River

Elbe River

The Alps, stretching more than 2,000 miles (3,200 km), is the most important mountain range in western Europe. The highest point, **Mont Blanc** (15,626 feet [4,808 m]), is on the border of France and Italy.

Dnieper River

Mount El'Brus, with an altitude of 18,337 ft (5,642 m), is the highest peak on the continent.

Alps

Danube River

Carpathians

2

Black Sea

40°N

Corsica

Italy, located close to where the Eurasian and African plates meet, experiences major volcanic activity, with Etna, Stromboli, and **Vesuvius**.

Sardinia

Sicily

Mount Etna

10°E

20°E

30°E

40°E

Asia

Earth's largest continent

Asia, which takes up four-fifths of Eurasia, is the largest region in the world (32 percent of the planet's landmass). Part of its relief is composed of very old shields: the Arabian and Indian peninsulas, bordering the Indian Ocean, and the Central Siberian Plateau. The steppes of Turkestan and the western Siberian plain are lowlands formed of sedimentary layers. The dominant feature of the landscape is the imposing mountain belt that crosses the continent from west to east (Hindu Kush, Himalayas), which extends into the Pacific Ocean to form Indonesia and the Philippines to the south, Japan and Kamchatka to the north.

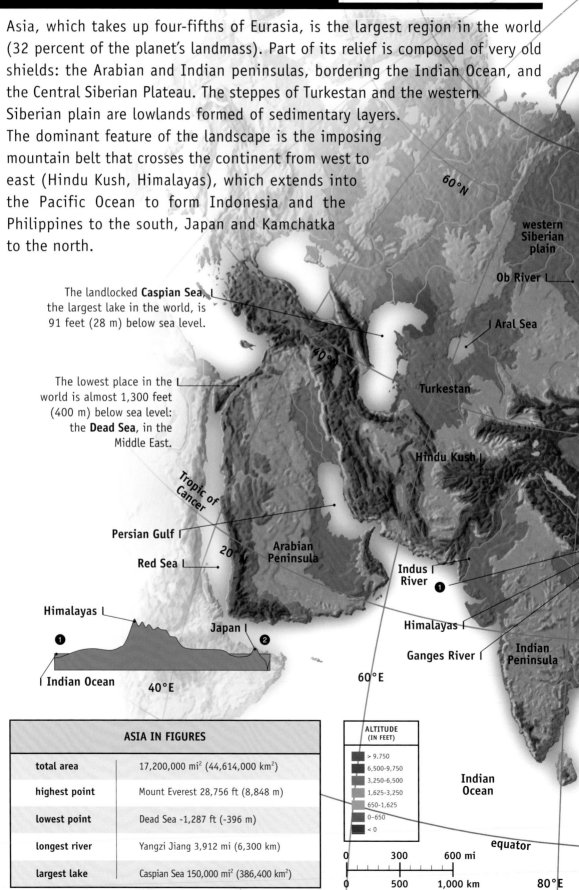

The landlocked **Caspian Sea**, the largest lake in the world, is 91 feet (28 m) below sea level.

The lowest place in the world is almost 1,300 feet (400 m) below sea level: the **Dead Sea**, in the Middle East.

60°N

western Siberian plain

Ob River

Aral Sea

40°

Turkestan

Hindu Kush

Tropic of Cancer

Persian Gulf

Red Sea

20° N

Arabian Peninsula

Indus River ❶

Himalayas

❶

Japan ❷

Indian Ocean

40°E

Himalayas

Ganges River

Indian Peninsula

60°E

Indian Ocean

equator

80°E

ASIA IN FIGURES	
total area	17,200,000 mi² (44,614,000 km²)
highest point	Mount Everest 28,756 ft (8,848 m)
lowest point	Dead Sea -1,287 ft (-396 m)
longest river	Yangzi Jiang 3,912 mi (6,300 km)
largest lake	Caspian Sea 150,000 mi² (386,400 km²)

ALTITUDE (IN FEET)	
	> 9,750
	6,500-9,750
	3,250-6,500
	1,625-3,250
	650-1,625
	0-650
	< 0

0   300   600 mi

0   500   1,000 km

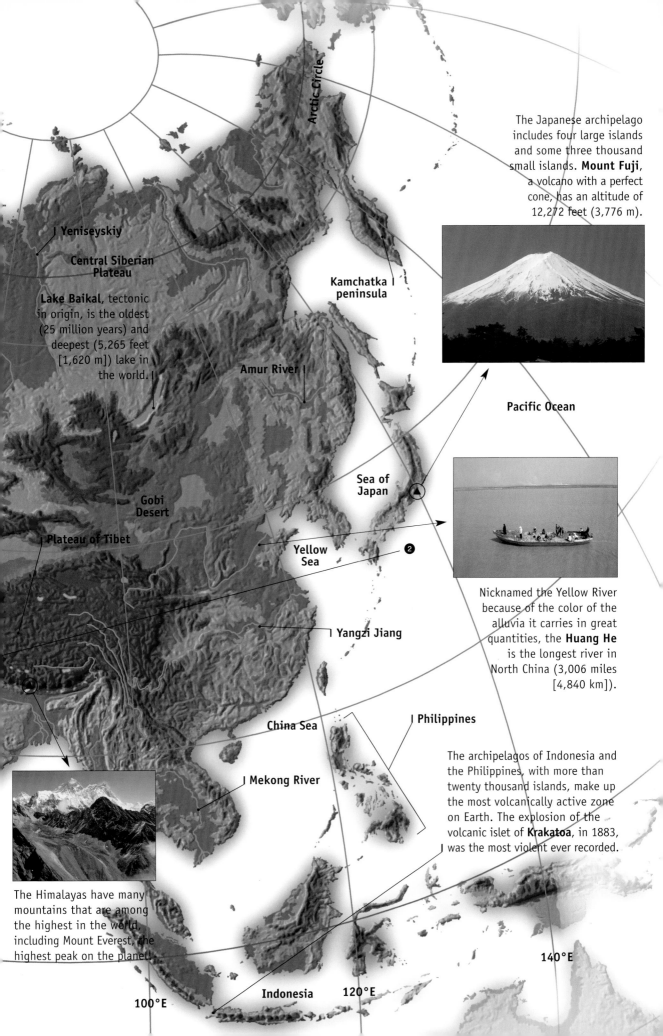

Yeniseyskiy

Central Siberian Plateau

Lake Baikal, tectonic in origin, is the oldest (25 million years) and deepest (5,265 feet [1,620 m]) lake in the world.

Kamchatka peninsula

Amur River

Gobi Desert

Plateau of Tibet

Sea of Japan

Yellow Sea

Yangzi Jiang

China Sea

Mekong River

Philippines

Indonesia

The Japanese archipelago includes four large islands and some three thousand small islands. **Mount Fuji**, a volcano with a perfect cone, has an altitude of 12,272 feet (3,776 m).

Pacific Ocean

Nicknamed the Yellow River because of the color of the alluvia it carries in great quantities, the **Huang He** is the longest river in North China (3,006 miles [4,840 km]).

The archipelagos of Indonesia and the Philippines, with more than twenty thousand islands, make up the most volcanically active zone on Earth. The explosion of the volcanic islet of **Krakatoa**, in 1883, was the most violent ever recorded.

The Himalayas have many mountains that are among the highest in the world, including Mount Everest, the highest peak on the planet.

100°E   120°E   140°E

Oceania

A multitude of islands in the Pacific

Unlike the other continents, Oceania is not a landmass surrounded by seas, but a great number of islands sprinkled in the Pacific and Indian oceans. With an area of 2,965,000 square miles (7,682,000 sq km), Australia is Oceania's true continent. The many islands surrounding it are grouped into three geographic ensembles: Melanesia, northeast of Australia, including Papua-New Guinea; Micronesia, to the north; and Polynesia, including all landmasses up to the mid-Pacific, including New Zealand. Oceania's total area represents 6 percent of Earth's landmass.

Gulf of Carpentaria

20°S

Great Sandy Desert

Indian Ocean

Great Victoria Desert

Lake Eyre

30°S

120°E

The strange sandstone monolith called **Ayers Rock** (2.24 miles [3.6 km] long) rises in the heart of the Australian desert.

Great Australian Bight

Australian desert

New Zealand

140°E

40°S

Murray River

Indian Ocean | Great Dividing Range | Tasman Sea

OCEANIA IN FIGURES	
total area	3,284,000 mi² (8,507,000 km²)
highest point	Mount Wilhelm 14,654 ft (4,509 m)
lowest point	Lake Eyre - 52 ft (-16 m)
longest river	Murray River 1,608 mi (2,589 km)
largest lake	Lake Eyre 3,600 mi² (9,300 km²)

ALTITUDE (IN FEET)	
	> 9,750
	6,500-9,750
	3,250-6,500
	1,625-3,250
	650-1,625
	0-650
	< 0

0   300   600 mi

0   500   1,000 km

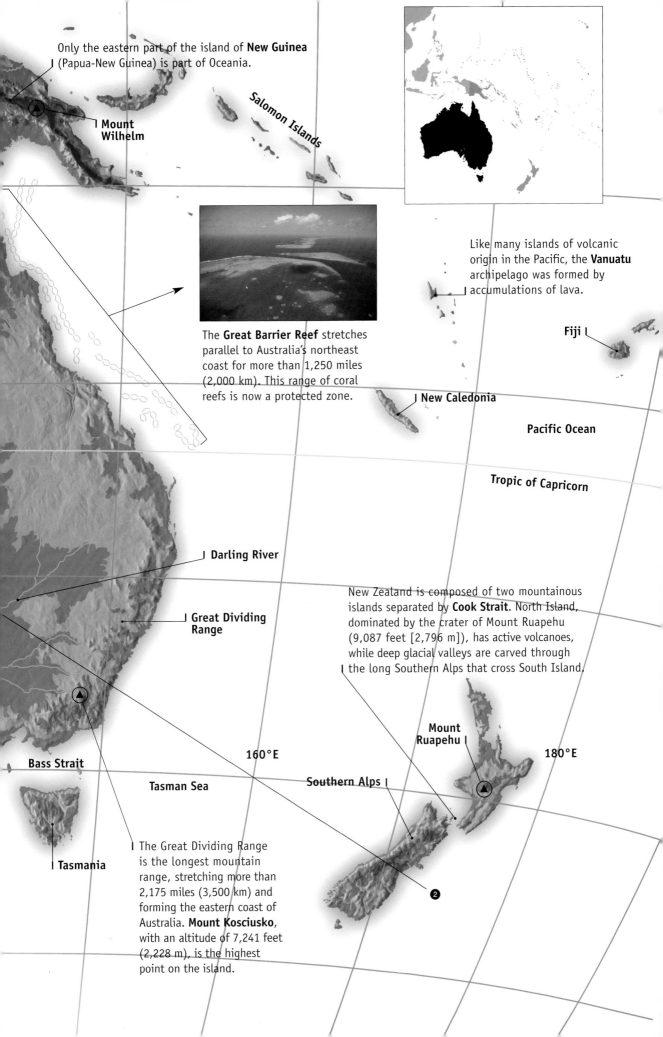

Only the eastern part of the island of **New Guinea** (Papua-New Guinea) is part of Oceania.

Mount Wilhelm

Salomon Islands

Like many islands of volcanic origin in the Pacific, the **Vanuatu** archipelago was formed by accumulations of lava.

The **Great Barrier Reef** stretches parallel to Australia's northeast coast for more than 1,250 miles (2,000 km). This range of coral reefs is now a protected zone.

Fiji

New Caledonia

Pacific Ocean

Tropic of Capricorn

Darling River

Great Dividing Range

New Zealand is composed of two mountainous islands separated by **Cook Strait**. North Island, dominated by the crater of Mount Ruapehu (9,087 feet [2,796 m]), has active volcanoes, while deep glacial valleys are carved through the long Southern Alps that cross South Island.

Mount Ruapehu

160°E

180°E

Bass Strait

Tasman Sea

Southern Alps

Tasmania

The Great Dividing Range is the longest mountain range, stretching more than 2,175 miles (3,500 km) and forming the eastern coast of Australia. **Mount Kosciusko**, with an altitude of 7,241 feet (2,228 m), is the highest point on the island.

❷

Africa

A flat continent edged with scarped relief

Africa is a massive continent with an area of 11,700,000 square miles (30,365,000 sq km), or 20 percent of the planet's landmass; the equator runs through its center. Most of Africa is composed of a very old platform that forms a continental plateau, and it is bounded by steep rectilinear coasts and very few islands. Mountain ranges are concentrated in the north (Atlas); south (Drakensberg); and east (Ethiopian Highlands), where they are shaped by a major rift system, the Great Rift Valley. The subequatorial zone, covered with forest and savanna, is irrigated by powerful rivers (Congo, Niger), while the subtropical regions contain deserts (Sahara, Namib, Kalahari) that have little natural irrigation.

With an area of more than 3 million square miles (8 million sq km), the **Sahara** is the largest desert in the world. It extends from the Atlantic Ocean to the Red Sea and covers all of North Africa.

10°W

0°

30°N

| Atlas

Tropic of Cancer

20°N

| Senegal River

10°N

Niger River |

Gulf of Guinea

equator

10°S

Atlantic Ocean

20°S

Tropic of Capricorn

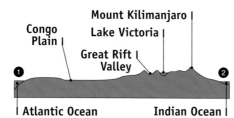

Mount Kilimanjaro |

Congo Plain |

Lake Victoria |

Great Rift Valley

① Atlantic Ocean |

② Indian Ocean |

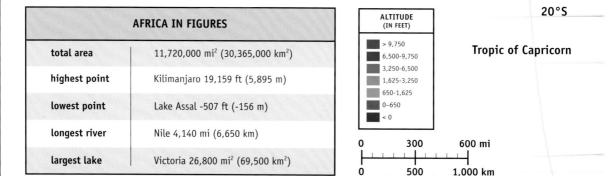

AFRICA IN FIGURES	
total area	11,720,000 mi² (30,365,000 km²)
highest point	Kilimanjaro 19,159 ft (5,895 m)
lowest point	Lake Assal -507 ft (-156 m)
longest river	Nile 4,140 mi (6,650 km)
largest lake	Victoria 26,800 mi² (69,500 km²)

ALTITUDE (IN FEET)	
	> 9,750
	6,500-9,750
	3,250-6,500
	1,625-3,250
	650-1,625
	0-650
	< 0

0   300   600 mi

0   500   1,000 km

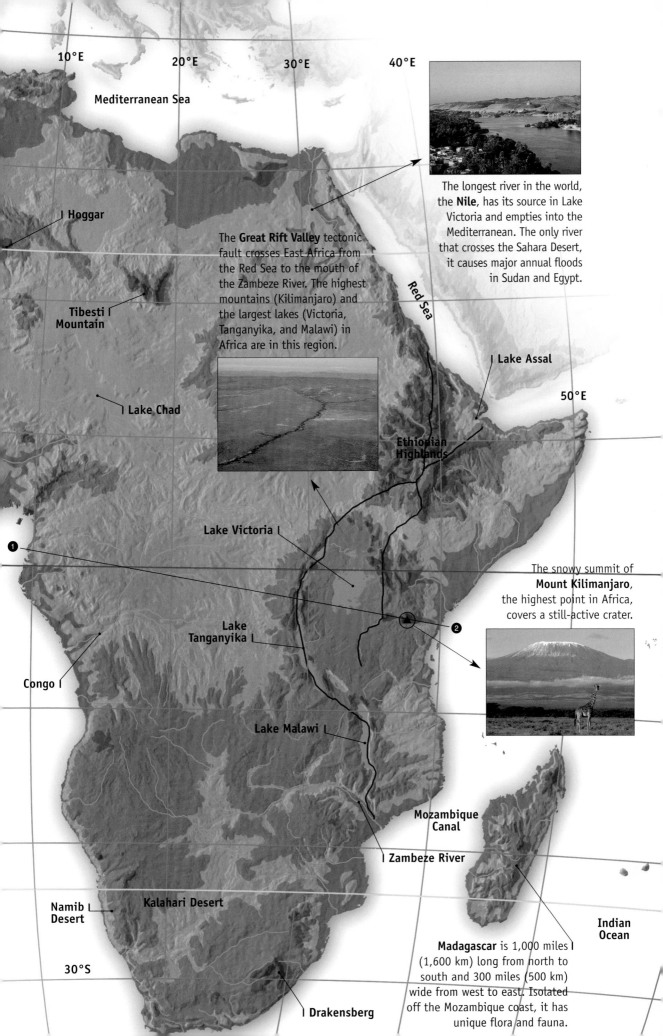

10°E   **20°E**   **30°E**   **40°E**

Mediterranean Sea

The longest river in the world, the **Nile**, has its source in Lake Victoria and empties into the Mediterranean. The only river that crosses the Sahara Desert, it causes major annual floods in Sudan and Egypt.

I Hoggar

The **Great Rift Valley** tectonic fault crosses East Africa from the Red Sea to the mouth of the Zambeze River. The highest mountains (Kilimanjaro) and the largest lakes (Victoria, Tanganyika, and Malawi) in Africa are in this region.

Red Sea

I Lake Assal

50°E

Tibesti Mountain I

I Lake Chad

Ethiopian Highlands

Lake Victoria I

❶

The snowy summit of **Mount Kilimanjaro**, the highest point in Africa, covers a still-active crater.

Lake Tanganyika I

❷

Congo I

Lake Malawi I

Mozambique Canal

Zambeze River

I Indian Ocean

Namib Desert I   Kalahari Desert

Madagascar is 1,000 miles (1,600 km) long from north to south and 300 miles (500 km) wide from west to east. Isolated off the Mozambique coast, it has unique flora and fauna.

30°S

I Drakensberg

Glossary

ablation: The process of erosion that reduces the size of a glacier.

alluvia: Solid materials (sand, gravel, silt, pebbles) transported and deposited by a watercourse.

altitude: Vertical distance from one point to a reference level, generally average sea level.

archipelago: A group of islands.

arete: A sharp crest of a mountain separating two glacial valleys.

atmospheric: Relating to the gaseous layer surrounding Earth.

bay: A relatively open part of a stretch of water or watercourse that makes an indentation into the land. Usually, a bay is smaller than a gulf.

cirque: A steep hollow, often containing a lake, that occurs at at the upper end of a mountain valley.

cordillera: A long, narrow mountain range in South America or Australia.

creep: The slow movement of rock, soil, and other debris down a weathered slope.

ice age: A geologic period during which glaciers covered much of Earth's landmass.

kettle: A depression or indentation left in a mass of glacial drift, probably formed by the melting of a block of glacial ice.

massif: A group of mountains, often made of ancient bedrock, that may take various shapes (such as plateaus, volcanic formations, or severely eroded elements).

monolith: A block of a single mass of rock.

moraine: An accumulation of rocks, stones, boulders, or other debris carried and deposited by a glacier.

plain: A vast stretch of relatively flat land, at a lower elevation than the relief features in the environs, with slightly hollowed valleys.

plateau: A relatively flat stretch of land distinguished from the surrounding plain by the deep, steep-sided valleys that form its boundaries and by its altitude, which is higher than that in the surrounding region.

polar circle: Imaginary lines on the 66°34' North (Arctic Circle) and South (Antarctic Circle) parallels. These lines mark the edge of the polar zones, where the day lasts twenty-four hours during the summer solstice and the Sun does not appear at all during the winter solstice.

projection: A system of intersecting lines, such as the grid on a map, on which part or all of the globe is represented as a flat surface.

relief: All unevenness (depressions and elevations) in the topographic surface of a region.

resolution: The number of points per unit of measurement detectable by the scanning of a measurement instrument. A high resolution indicates that the instrument used has great optical sensitivity.

sediments: Solid mineral materials (rock, sand, mud) that have been scraped away from their original location and transported by water, ice, or wind to be deposited in another location. Organic materials may also form sediments.

solstice: The two times of the year when the Sun is farthest from the plane of the equator, corresponding to the shortest day (winter solstice) and the longest day (summer solstice).

talus: A slope formed by the accumulation of debris, especially at the bottom of a cliff.

topology: The study of a place in relation to its physical features, usually as found on a map, and its history.

ultrasound: Sonar vibration with too high a frequency to be perceptible by the human ear (more than 20,000 hertz).

watercourse: A waterway; the bed or channel created by a waterway.

Books

The Discoverers: A History of Man's Search to Know His World and Himself. Daniel J. Boorstin (Vintage Books)

Don't Know Much About Geography: Everything You Need to Know about the World but Never Learned. Kenneth Charles Davis (William Morrow and Company)

In Suspect Terrain. John A. McPhee (Farrar, Straus and Giroux, Inc.)

Into Thin Air: A Personal Account of the Mount Everest Disaster (The Illustrated Edition). Jon Krakauer (Anchor Books)

Longitude: The True Story of a Lone Genius Who Solved the Greatest Scientific Problem of His Time. Dava Sobel (Viking Penguin)

Mavericks: The Story of Big-Wave Surfing. Matt Warshaw (Chronicle Books)

Merriam Webster's Geographical Dictionary. (Merriam-Webster)

The New Geography: How the Digital Revolution is Reshaping the American Landscape. Joel Kotkin (Random House)

Photo Archive of Famous Places of the World. Donald M. Witte, editor (Dover Publications, Inc.)

Prince Henry "the Navigator": A Life. Peter E. Russell (Yale University Press)

The Story of Maps. Lloyd A. Brown (Dover Publications)

Videos

Grand Canyon: The Hidden Secrets. Keith Merrill (Sling Shot)

The Great Barrier Reef. George Casey (Sling Shot)

Himalayan River Run (National Geographic Video)

The Inland Sea. Donald Carrie (Image Entertainment)

Mount Everest: The Fatal Climb (American Home Treasures)

Zion Canyon: Treasure of the Gods. Keith Merrill (Sling Shot)

Web Sites

Fascinating World of Maps and Mapping
oddens.geog.uu.nl/index.html

900 Geography & History
www.ultranet.com/~greenvil/ Childrens_Webpage/Child900.htm

Nice Geography Sites
www.frw.ruu.nl/nicegeo.html

Matt Rosenberg Geography: Homework Help
geography.about.com/science/geograp hy/cs/homeworkhelp/index.htm

Index

Index